L WHO
ORNET'S NEST

ANTONIO FUSO
AND PATRICIA MULVIHILL
COVER BY LEE BERMEJO
HE HORNET'S NEST BY STIEG LARSSON

W9-AXZ-322

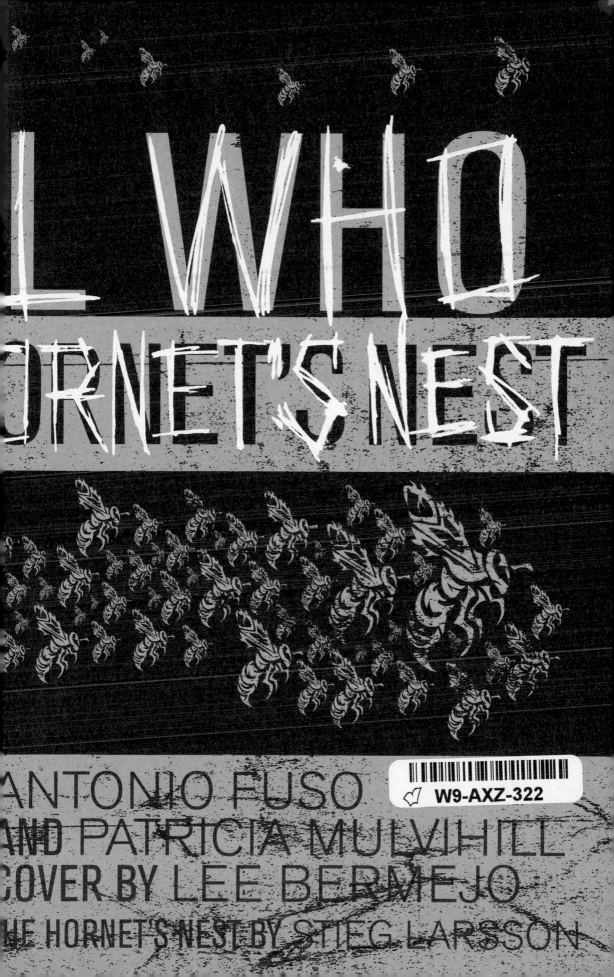

Will Dennis Jamie S. Rich Editors Greg Lockard Associate Editor Sara Miller Molly Mahan Assistant Editors Steve Cook Design Director – Books Louis Prandi Publication Desig

Shelly Bond VP & Executive Editor – Vertig

Diane Nelson President Dan DiDio and Jim Lee Co-Publishers Geoff Johns Chief Creative Officer Amit Desai Senior VP – Marketing & Global Franchise Managemen
Nairi Gardiner Senior VP – Finance Sam Ades VP – Digital Marketing Bobbie Chase VP – Talent Development Mark Chiarello Senior VP – Art, Design & Collected Edition
John Cunningham VP – Content Strategy Anne DePies VP – Strategy Planning & Reporting Don Falletti VP – Manufacturing Operation
Lawrence Ganem VP – Editorial Administration & Talent Relations Alison Gill Senior VP – Manufacturing & Operation
Hank Kanalz Senior VP – Editorial Strategy & Administration Jay Kogan VP – Legal Affairs Derek Maddalena Senior VP – Sales & Business Developmen
Jack Mahan VP – Business Affairs Dan Miron VP – Sales Planning & Trade Development Nick Napolitano VP – Manufacturing Administratio
Carol Roeder VP – Marketing Eddie Scannell VP – Mass Account & Digital Sales Courtney Simmons Senior VP – Publicity & Communication
Jim (Ski) Sokolowski VP – Comic Book Specialty & Newsstand Sales Sandy Yi Senior VP – Global Franchise Managemen

THE GIRL WHO KICKED THE HORNET'S NEST Published by DC Comics, 2900 West Alameda Ave., Burbank, CA 91522 A Warner Bros. Entertainment Company. Copyright © 2015 Moggliden AB. All Rights Reserved. Based on the novel THE GIR WHO KICKED THE HORNET'S NEST by Stieg Larsson. The Girl Who Kicked the Hornet's Nest names, characters and all related elements are trademarks of Moggliden AB. VERTIGO is a trademark of DC Comics. The stories, characters and inciden mentioned in this book are entirely fictional. DC Comics does not read or accept unsolicited submissions of ideas, stories or artwork. DC Comics, a Warner Bros. Entertainment Company. Printed in the USA. First Printing. ISBN: 978-1-4012-6477-

MIX
Paper from responsible sources
FSC® C101537
www.fsc.org

Library of Congress Cataloging-in-Publication Data

Mina, Denise, author.
The girl who kicked the hornet's nest / adapted by Denise Mina ; art by Antonio Fuso and Andrea Mutti.
pages cm
ISBN 978-1-4012-6477-2

1. Crime--Sweden--Comic books, strips, etc. 2. Murder—Investigatio -Comic books, strips, etc. 3. Graphic novels. I. Fuso, Antonio, illustrato II. Mutti, Andrea, 1973- illustrator. III. Larsson, Stieg, 1954-2004. Gi who kicked the hornet's nest IV. Title
PN6737.M57G55 201
741.5'942—dc2
201500717

VERTIGO

THE GIR

KICKED THE H

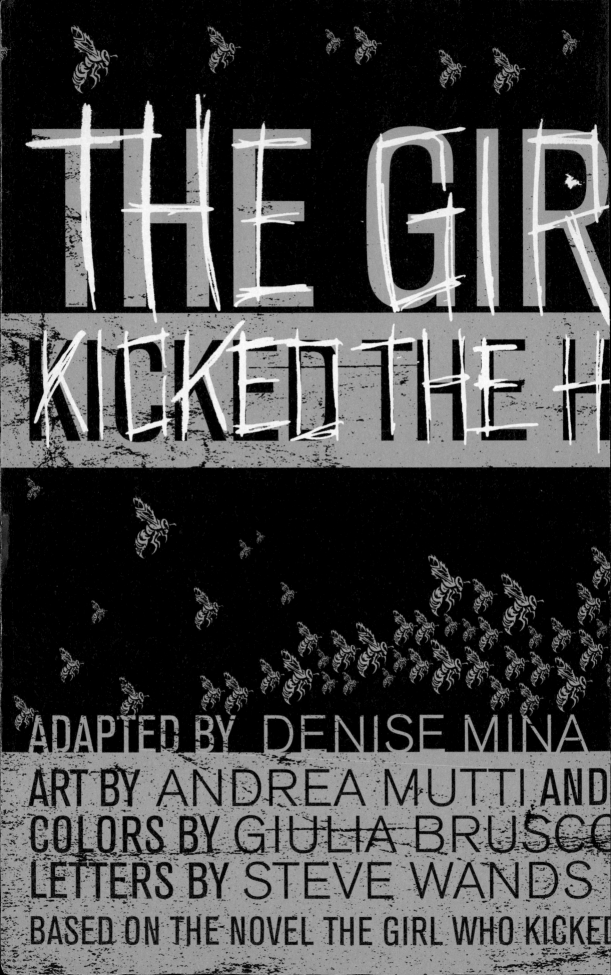

ADAPTED BY DENISE MINA

ART BY ANDREA MUTTI AND

COLORS BY GIULIA BRUSCO

LETTERS BY STEVE WANDS

BASED ON THE NOVEL THE GIRL WHO KICKE

DR. JONASSON!
WE'VE GOT TWO COMING IN BY AIR.
A MULTIPLE BULLET WOUNDS AND AN AXE IN THE FACE.
JAN, IF YOU WOULDN'T MIND PAGING DR. HOLM, PLEASE.

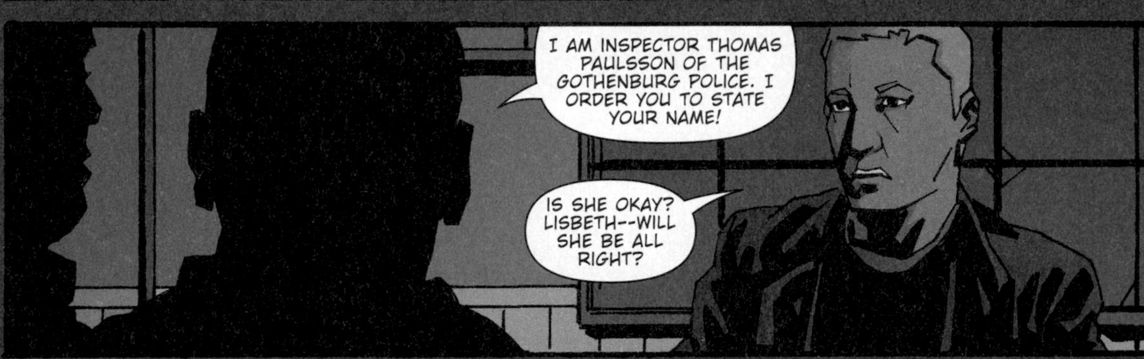
I AM INSPECTOR THOMAS PAULSSON OF THE GOTHENBURG POLICE. I ORDER YOU TO STATE YOUR NAME!
IS SHE OKAY? LISBETH--WILL SHE BE ALL RIGHT?

NAME!
BLOMKVIST, MIKAEL--
THE *JOURNALIST* MIKAEL BLOMKVIST?
WHAT ARE YOU DOING HERE?

I FOLLOWED LISBETH HERE. I WAS AFRAID FOR HER SAFETY.
BY THE TIME I ARRIVED SHE WAS SHOT AND LYING ON THIS BENCH--THERE'S A MAN, RONALD NIEDERMANN, I HIT HIM WITH MY CAR, HE'S TIED TO A ROAD SIGN AT THE TURN-OFF FOR THE MAIN ROAD...

I ARREST YOU FOR MURDER--!
HE'S NOT DEAD.
--ATTEMPTED MURDER!
HE RAN IN FRONT OF MY CAR.
HE HAS KILLED THREE PEOPLE--
TORSTENSSON: TAKE INGEMARSSON, GET DOWN THERE AND MAKE SURE THAT MAN IS ALL RIGHT.
YOU DON'T UNDERSTAND.
HE'S NOT NORMAL...
YOU DON'T UNDERSTAND.
ABOUT NIEDERMANN.
HE'S KILLED...
DROP THE GUN! DROP THE GUN!
NO!
DON'T SEND THEM ON THEIR OWN!
THEY NEED BACK-UP.

WHY DID THEY LET HIM COME BACK FROM MEDICAL LEAVE?
GOD KNOWS.
HE'S NOT WELL. ANY IDIOT COULD TELL THAT.
MUST HAVE PUT ON A GOOD SHOW ON THE DAY. IT'S ONLY ONE INTERVIEW.

HOLY CRAP!
LOOK AT THIS POOR BASTARD!

MOOSE CROSSING

NIEDERMANN'S AN ANIMAL! TWO OFFICERS ARE NOT ENOUGH!
WE'VE FOUND HIM, SIR. OVER.

DON'T APPROACH HIM!
CHECK TO SEE IF HE NEEDS MEDICAL ATTENTION AND REPORT BACK. OVER.

WHY DID YOU BRING THE GUN HERE?
A FINE STORY.
I DIDN'T. I *FOUND* IT HERE.
LOOK: *I* CALLED *YOU*.
WHAT BETTER COVER FOR THE ATTACKER?
LISBETH HAS BEEN FRAMED FOR A DOUBLE MURDER IN STOCKHOLM. SHE CAME HERE TO CLEAR HER NAME. THEY TRIED TO KILL HER!
OR SHE TRIED TO KILL THEM. WHAT BETTER MOTIVE COULD ANYONE HAVE?
SHE WILL BE CHARGED *IF*, AND WHEN, SHE REGAINS CONSCIOUSNESS.
GET BUBLANSKI ON THE PHONE!
JAN BUBLANSKI OF THE STOCKHOLM POLICE.
I DON'T KNOW WHAT YOU'VE BEEN TOLD, MR. BLOMKVIST. BUT EVEN A FAMOUS JOURNALIST DOESN'T GET TO CHOOSE THE POLICE WHO INVESTIGATE THEM.
YOU NEED SOME BACKGROUND ON THIS CASE. YOU DON'T KNOW WHAT YOU'RE DEALING WITH--
SPPPSP. HELL...SPSS... HELLSPS. **HELP US.**

HMM.
BAD.
THE BULLET HAS TURNED: WE CAN'T EVEN PULL IT STRAIGHT OUT THROUGH THE ENTRY PATH.
...BONE FRAGMENTS *EVERYWHERE*.
THE OLD MAN'S IN BETTER SHAPE THAN HER.
DID YOU RECOGNIZE HER FROM THE PAPERS?
I DON'T READ THE PAPERS.
JAN, YOU COULDN'T MISS HER: HER PICTURE'S BEEN EVERYWHERE FOR SIX MONTHS. SHE'S THAT LESBIAN SATANIST THEY'VE BEEN SEARCHING FOR.
THE ONE WANTED FOR ALL THE MURDERS?
YES, *THAT* LESBIAN SATANIST.
I DON'T KNOW IF SHE'LL BE WORSHIPPING ANYTHING AFTER WE'VE GOT ALL THIS OUT.

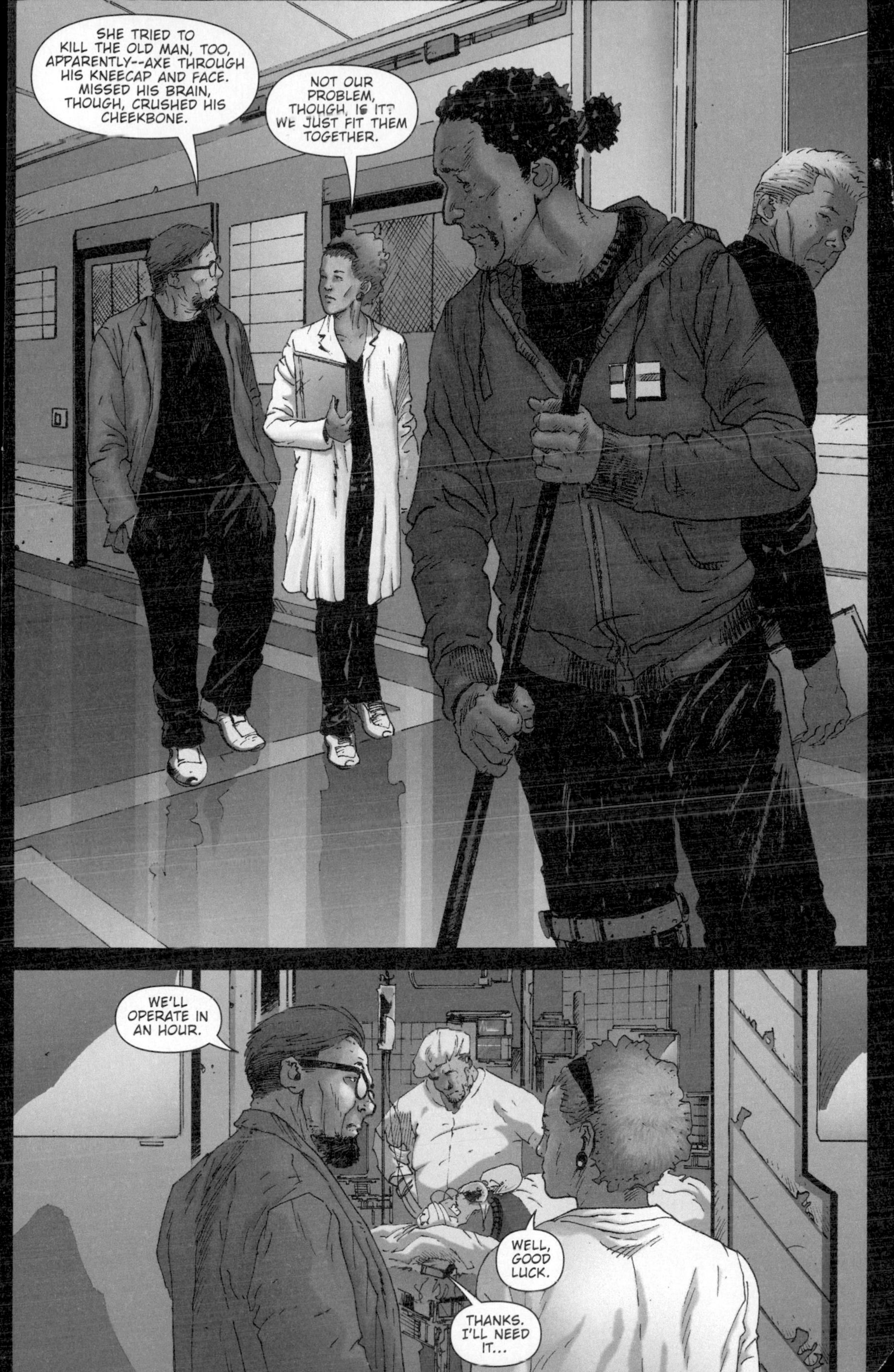
SHE TRIED TO KILL THE OLD MAN, TOO, APPARENTLY--AXE THROUGH HIS KNEECAP AND FACE. MISSED HIS BRAIN, THOUGH, CRUSHED HIS CHEEKBONE.
NOT OUR PROBLEM, THOUGH, IS IT? WE JUST FIT THEM TOGETHER.
WE'LL OPERATE IN AN HOUR.
WELL, GOOD LUCK.
THANKS. I'LL NEED IT...

MOOSE
CROSSING

TORSTENSSON! OFFICER TORSTENSSON! ANSWER ME!

YOU HAVE GOT TO PHONE BUBLANSKI!
NIEDERMANN IS INCREDIBLY DANGEROUS. YOU CAN'T LET HIM GET AWAY.
--CAR'S GONE, SIR. OVER.

SIR--
I AM ARRESTING YOU FOR POSSESSION OF AN ILLEGAL WEAPON--
HE'LL KILL SOMEONE ELSE. PHONE BUBLANSKI!
SIR-- INSPECTOR MARCUS ERLAND ON THE PHONE FOR YOU.
WHAT'S GOING ON OVER THERE, PAULSSON?

04:03

ZSSB ZSSB ZSSB

CENTRALSTATION

SJ

SJ 2000

GÖTEBORG

05:10 am

5

NURSERY NURSE.
THAT'S THE WORST YET, HOLMBERG.

WHAT DO YOU THINK I SHOULD RETRAIN AS, THEN?
THAT'S NOT A JOB.
WHINY GIT.
BUT IT'S WHAT YOU'RE GOOD AT.

GOOD BLOOD PRESSURE.
PATIENT VERY FIT AND BLOOD LOSS MITIGATED BY THE APPLICATION OF DUCT TAPE OVER HER WOUNDS.
YEAH, GOOD FIELD DRESSING. DID THE POLICE DO THAT?
NO, THINK IT WAS THE MAN WHO FOUND HER.
MIKAEL BLOMKVIST, YOU HEARD OF HIM?
NO. I WANT THE FRAGMENTS COUNTED AS THEY COME OUT.
THERE SHOULD BE THIRTY-TWO.
TWENTY-SEVEN SO FAR...

INSPECTOR ERLANDER?!
PLEASE RETURN TO HEADQUARTERS, INSPECTOR PAULSSON.

WHO ARE YOU?
I AM CRIMINAL INSPECTOR ERLANDER.
YOU ARE MIKAEL BLOMKVIST?

MR. BLOMKVIST, I HAVE KNOWN INSPECTOR BUBLANSKI FOR TWENTY YEARS.
HE TELLS ME THAT YOU ARE A "JOURNALIST AND A BASTARD."
...BUT YOU MIGHT JUST KNOW WHAT IS GOING ON HERE.

PERHAPS YOU COULD TELL ME WHAT YOU THINK HAS HAPPENED...

DAG AND MIA, TWO COLLEAGUES OF OURS, WERE SHOT IN STOCK-HOLM. IT LOOKED LIKE SALANDER BUT IT WASN'T.
IT WAS NIEDERMANN.
BUBBLE SAID THAT.
--WITH THE COLT YOU WAVED AT PAULSSON?
I WAS TRYING TO HAND IT IN...
PAULSSON HASN'T HANDLED THIS VERY WELL. BUT HE'S NOT HERE NOW.
NEITHER IS NIEDERMANN.
NEITHER IS OFFICER TORSTENSSON.
WHAT DID HE DO TO HIM?
BROKE HIS ***NECK***. I KNEW HIM... TELL ME ABOUT ***KARL AXEL BODIN***.
HIS REAL NAME IS ZALACHENKO. HE'S A RUSSIAN DEFECTOR.
HE'S BEEN PROTECTED BY SAPO WHILE RUNNING A CRIMINAL NETWORK.
WHY WOULD THE SECRET SERVICE PROTECT HIM WHILE HE DID THAT?
TO COVER THEIR BACKS SO THE RUSSIANS DIDN'T KNOW.

WHAT'S SALANDER'S CONNECTION?
HE'S HER FATHER. SHE SET FIRE TO HIS CAR, WITH HIM ***IN*** IT, WHEN SHE WAS TWELVE.
SHE'S BEEN HELD IN PSYCHIATRIC UNITS EVER SINCE. UNFAIRLY, I MIGHT ADD.

WE'RE GOING TO HAVE TO CHARGE HER WITH ATTEMPTED MURDER.
YOU COULDN'T BE MORE WRONG.
HE'S GOT AN AXE IN HIS FACE, MR. BLOMKVIST. IT *IS* ATTEMPTED MURDER.
IT'S SELF-DEFENSE.
IS THAT WHY SHE TRACKED HIM DOWN AND CAME AFTER HIM?
WE'VE GOT VIDEO EVIDENCE OF HER HIDING IN THE BUSHES FOR EIGHT HOURS, WATCHING THE HOUSE. IF THAT'S NOT INTENT, I DON'T KNOW WHAT IS.
SHE KNEW NIEDERMANN WAS HERE.
SHE WANTED TO CONFRONT HER FATHER ABOUT ***NIEDERMANN***.
NOT KILL HIM.
AND THE AXE IN THE FACE WAS A MISTAKE?
HAVE YOU SEEN THE GRAVE OUTSIDE?
THE BIG HOLE OUTSIDE THAT'S FULL OF BLOOD?
TEST IT. THAT WILL BE HER BLOOD.
NIEDERMANN KIDNAPPED A WOMAN CALLED MIRIAM WU.
HE TRIED TO TORTURE HER IN A WAREHOUSE AND THEN BURNT IT DOWN.
THE POLICE HAVE FOUND THREE GRAVES ON THE GROUNDS THAT MATCH THE ONE OUTSIDE.
HARD TO BELIEVE...
...BUT THEN THE TRUTH OFTEN IS.

– LISBETH SALANDER AT A FARM IN GOSSEBERGA THIS MORNING. INITIAL REPORT STATES THAT ONE POLICE OFFICER HAS BEEN KILLED AND A SECOND CRITICALLY INJURED.
breaking NEWS
1 MISSED CALL
ANNIKA, IT'S ME.
JUST LETTING YOU KNOW: I THINK I'VE FOUND LISBETH.
I'M HEADING TO GOSSEBERGA.
MIKEY, MIKEY, PICK UP.
PLEASE, MIKEY.
TO LEAVE A MESSAGE, SPEAK AFTER THE TONE.

THANKS FOR COMING.
INSPECTOR BUBLANSKI ORDERED US HERE, SIR.
MR. BLOMKVIST HAS TOLD ME THE BACKGROUND TO THE CASE.

I DOUBT THAT.
WHAT DO YOU MEAN?
YOU'VE BEEN HOLDING A LOT BACK, HAVEN'T YOU, MR. BLOMKVIST?
I DIDN'T SAY IT WAS THE *WHOLE* TRUTH.

DID HE TELL YOU HOW HE GOT HOLD OF BJÖRCK'S COPY OF THE 1991 PSYCHIATRIC REPORT ON SALANDER?
I'M AFRAID I DIDN'T ASK HIM.
HOW DID YOU GET HOLD OF IT?

I FOUND THAT COPY IN HER SECRET FLAT, WHICH I INTEND TO KEEP SECRET.
I'LL LET YOU HAVE IT BECAUSE I KNOW IT'S RELEVANT TO THE CASE.
IT'S NOT FOR YOU TO DECIDE WHAT *IS* AND *ISN'T* RELEVANT, MR. BLOMKVIST.

IT IS FOR ME TO DECIDE WHAT WILL KEEP LISBETH SAFE THOUGH.
SAFE FROM THE SECURITY SERVICES, INSPECTOR ERLANDER.
SAFE FROM US? YOU CAN'T DO THAT.
WERE YOU GOING TO TELL US BJURMAN RAPED HER?

HOW DO YOU KNOW THAT?
WHY DIDN'T YOU TELL US?
HOW COULD YOU KNOW THAT?

BJURMAN HAD A BIG TATTOO ON HIS BELLY. BADLY DONE. VERY DEEP AND UNEVEN.
"I AM A RAPIST."

DID SHE?!
WE'RE ASSUMING IT WAS HER.
I THINK YOU'RE ASSUMING RIGHT.

DID SHE TELL YOU SHE TATTOOED HIM?

--DIDN'T EVEN TELL ME HE RAPED HER.
WITH LISBETH YOU HAVE TO WORK THINGS OUT.
MAJOR TRUST ISSUES.

YOU WANT ME TO CHARGE HER?

WITH DAG AND MIA AND BJURMAN'S MURDERS.

WHAT ABOUT THE KIDNAPPING OF MIRIAM WU?

WELL ***OBVIOUSLY*** SHE DIDN'T DO THAT...

OBVIOUSLY THAT WAS RONALD NIEDERMANN, WHO IS RESPONSIBLE FOR THE THREE DEAD PEOPLE WHO WERE BURIED BEHIND THE WAREHOUSE. ***COINCIDENTALLY.***

ANOTHER COINCIDENCE: BJÖRK, A SÄPO AGENT, HAS BEEN RAPING YOUNG GIRLS AND SHE FOUND OUT ABOUT IT...

LET IT GO, BUBLANSKI.

SO, TAKE ME OFF THE CASE IF YOU WANT, BUT HE'S THERE NOW AND HE'S ARRESTING BJÖRCK.

TAKING ME OFF WON'T MAKE ANY DIFFERENCE IN THAT.

WILL YOU LET ME KNOW WHEN SHE GETS OUT OF SURGERY?
I'M FINE, ANNIKA.
YES, IT MUST HAVE BEEN, BUT YOU DON'T NEED TO **WORRY** NOW.
THEY'RE COMING FOR HER, ANNIKA, I CAN FEEL IT.
I'M NOT A CRIMINAL LAWYER, MIKEY.
SHE'S GOING TO NEED MORE THAN A CRIMINAL LAWYER. TO HAVE ANY CHANCE AT ALL, IT NEEDS TO BE A HUMAN RIGHTS ARGUMENT.
WILL YOU REPRESENT HER?
I JUST DON'T THINK I'M RIGHT FOR IT, MIKEY.
THEY'RE CIRCLING, ANNIKA.
I DON'T KNOW IF I CAN SAVE HER THIS TIME.

GUNNAR BJÖRCK.
I'M ARRESTING YOU FOR PAYING FOR SEXUAL SERVICES.
YOU'RE JOKING?

YOU CAN'T ARREST ME.
WHO AUTHORIZED THIS?
I THINK, AND I COULD BE WRONG, BUT YOU'RE JUST ABOUT TO ASK ME IF I KNOW WHO YOU ARE.

WHO SENT YOU TO DO THIS?
YOU'RE JUST A CRAZY--
YOU DON'T HAVE ANY AUTHORITY, DO YOU?

INSPECTOR JAN BUBLANSKI HAS AUTHORIZED THIS ARREST.
CALL THE OFFICE IF YOU LIKE.
OR CALL A LAWYER.

AS SOON AS WE GET INTO THE STATION, I'LL BE RELEASED.
YOU KNOW THAT, DON'T YOU?
YOU THINK SÄPO GIVE A SHIT ABOUT YOU?
NO. BUT THEY CAN'T AFFORD TO LET THIS GO TO COURT.
YOU'LL ALL GET DISCIPLINED.
YOU'VE NO IDEA OF THE TROUBLE THEY CAN CAUSE YOU.
SO YOU'RE SAYING WE SHOULDN'T ARREST YOU.
BECAUSE IT'S THE ***RIGHT*** THING TO DO.
BUT IT WON'T GO WELL FOR US?
YOU'RE WALKING INTO A SHITSTORM.
THAT'S THE DIFFERENCE BETWEEN THE POLICE AND THE SECURITY SERVICES.
OUR JOB IS WALKING INTO SHITSTORMS.
YOUR JOB IS COVERING THEM UP.

...FROM TWENTY OR SO YEARS AGO.
SUSPECT WAS A BOXER IN A GYM IN GERMANY.
WE ACTUALLY GOT THIS PHOTO FROM PAOLO ROBERTO.
BOXING
DRESDEN
-NIEDERMANN-
HE GUESSED HE WAS A BOXER AND PUT THE WORD OUT TO GYMS ALL OVER EUROPE.
HE HAS A CONDITION THAT MAKES HIM UNABLE TO FEEL ***PAIN***. VERY DANGEROUS FOR A BOXER, APPARENTLY.
UNFORTUNATELY, BECAUSE OF THAT CONDITION, HE WAS REFUSED MEMBERSHIP IN ANY BOXING BODY.
...SO WE HAVE NO ***MORE*** RECENT PHOTOGRAPHS.
-NIEDERMANN-
MIRIAM WU SAYS IT LOOKS NOTHING LIKE HIM ***NOW***.
I KNOW, AND THAT'S A REAL SHAME.
HE'S SPENT EIGHT MINUTES INFORMING THE ROOM THAT WE DON'T REALLY KNOW WHAT NIEDERMANN LOOKS LIKE.
HE KILLED AN OFFICER THIS MORNING.
WHERE IS HE ***NOW?***

HE'S HEADING FOR STOCKHOLM.
HE WAS HEADING EAST BUT MAY HAVE DOUBLED BACK.
HE'S FROM GERMANY ORIGINALLY SO IT MAKES SENSE FOR HIM TO HEAD BACK THERE.

THE PRESS ARE GOING TO ASK:
HOW DID THOSE TWO OFFICERS END UP GOING DOWN THERE ON THEIR OWN?

IN A WORD: ***PAULSSON.***

OH FUCK.
OH NO.
CHRIST, NOT THAT IDIOT.

THOMAS PAULSSON HAS BEEN OFF ON MEDICAL LEAVE.
I'M AFRAID E WAS ON A LOT F MEDICATION, A ACT HE HID FROM HE FITNESS-TO-SERVE REVIEW BOARD.
HE'S BEEN TAKEN OFF THE ROTATION NOW.
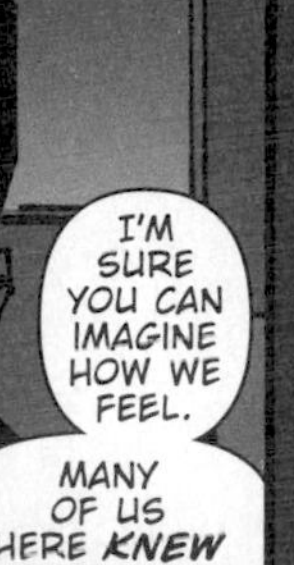
I'M SURE YOU CAN IMAGINE HOW WE FEEL.
MANY OF US HERE ***KNEW*** TORSTENSSON.

WE'VE GOT ONE OF THOSE IN OUR OFFICE.
YEAH.
AND WE'RE VERY SORRY FOR THE LOSS OF YOUR COLLEAGUE.

WE'RE HAPPY FOR INSPECTOR BUBLANSKI'S DIVISION TO INTERVIEW KARL AXEL BODIN WHEN HE REGAINS CONSCIOUSNESS.

INSPECTOR ERLANDER?

JAN?

CALL, SIR, FROM THE POLICE AT FLODA TRAIN STATION.

NIEDERMANN?

SHE'S A NURSE.

DROPPED HER KID AT NURSERY.

IT'S AROUND THE CORNER FROM FLODA STATION.

SHE'S BEEN MISSING FOR TWO HOURS NOW.

DRIVING A DARK BLUE RENAULT.

SHIT.

WE'VE GOT AN APB OUT ON THE CAR.

WE CAN'T WAIT FOR BUBLANSKI TO GET HER.

YOU TWO GO AND SPEAK TO KARL BODIN NOW.

SEE IF YOU CAN GET ANY INFORMATION OUT OF HIM ABOUT NIEDERMANN'S WHEREABOUTS.

MILLENNIUM MAGAZINE OFFICES.
BERGER
BERGER
I KNEW IT!
I KNEW YOU WEREN'T WORKING IN HERE! YOU'VE BEEN HIDING BEHIND THE DOOR FOR DAYS, RICKY.
WHAT THE HELL IS WRONG?
SHITSHIT SHIT.
I WANTED TO TELL MIKAEL FIRST.
I'VE BEEN PUTTING IT OFF.
WHAT IS IT?
I'VE BEEN APPOINTED EDITOR IN CHIEF OF SVENSKA MORGON-POSTEN.
I'M LEAVING MILLENNIUM.

RICKY THAT'S GREAT.
I START IN THREE DAYS.
THAT'S LESS GREAT, BUT THE JOB WILL BE GREAT.
MIKEY AND I SET THIS MAGAZINE UP TOGETHER...
I'M CALLING A STAFF MEETING.
YOU NEED TO TELL EVERYONE NOW.
I KNOW.
...I'LL BE PACKING MY DESK AND LEAVING TONIGHT.
I WON'T BE TAKING ANY ONGOING INVESTIGATIONS WITH ME.
NOT EVEN SALANDER?
NOT EVEN THAT. YOU NEED TO APPOINT A NEW EDITOR-IN-CHIEF AND I'M STILL A SHAREHOLDER.
SO I'LL LEAVE YOU TO IT.
WHAT ABOUT MIKAEL?
GOD NO, HE DISAPPEARS WHEN HE'S ON A STORY.
WELL, YOU'RE THE DEPUTY ED. YOU DO IT.
GOD NO!
NO WAY!

ALEXANDER ZALACHENKO.
MY NAME IS KARL AXEL BODIN.
YOUR NAME IS ZALACHENKO.
YOU'RE A RUSSIAN DEFECTOR.
YOU'RE A FUCKING WHORE COP-BITCH.
LISBETH SALANDER IS YOUR DAUGHTER.
THIS ISN'T THE FIRST TIME SHE HAS TRIED TO KILL ME.
WHY CAN'T THEY KEEP THAT BITCH LOCKED UP?
SHE KEEPS TRYING...

SHE IS RESPONSIBLE FOR THESE BURNS, DID YOU KNOW THAT?
SHE TRIED TO KILL ME WHEN SHE WAS *TWELVE*. SHE'S MENTALLY ILL.
WHERE IS SHE NOW?
YOU BEAT HER MOTHER UNTIL SHE WAS BRAIN DAMAGED.
THE POLICE DID NOTHING.
SO SHE THREW A MOLOTOV COCKTAIL INTO YOUR CAR.
THIS PAIN IS OVERWHELMING...
I'LL EXPLAIN: SALANDER'S MOTHER WAS A PROSTITUTE, A WHORE. *ANYONE* COULD HAVE BEATEN HER.
LISBETH *DECIDED* IT WAS ME.
IS LISBETH IN THIS HOSPITAL?
WE NEED INFORMATION ABOUT NIEDERMANN--
I'VE BEEN ATTACKED...I'M IN TERRIBLE PAIN...
I'M A VICTIM HERE, AS MUCH AS ANYONE ELSE. I'M JUST A *DEFENSELESS* OLD MAN, DISABLED...
CAN'T YOU GET THIS FUCKING WHORE OFF MY BACK?
RONALD NIEDERMANN MURDERED A POLICE OFFICER THIS MORNING.

I HIRED HIM TO PROTECT ME!
FROM THAT SALANDER BITCH!
I'M A HELPLESS OLD MAN!
I ADMIT IT: I HAVE BEEN WORRIED ABOUT NIEDERMANN FOR SOME TIME.
HE'S ERRATIC, MOODY. I'VE BEEN WORRIED BY HIS BEHAVIOR.
I WILL BE HONEST WITH YOU BOTH.
I'M AFRAID OF HIM.
YOU'RE A LYING BAST--
--TERRIBLY AFRAID. I SUSPECT THAT HE'S VIOLENT.
WHERE WOULD HE GO?
A POOR OLD MAN LIKE ME. I'VE NEVER, EVER BEEN ARRESTED.
DID YOU KNOW THAT?
WHERE WOULD NIEDERMANN HIDE?
I DON'T REALLY KNOW HIM.
YOU WON'T HELP US FIND HIM?
I WANT SALANDER CHARGED WITH ATTEMPTING TO MURDER ME.
I WANT THAT BITCH PUT AWAY FOR THE REST OF HER WORTHLESS FUCKING LIFE.

LISSSSBETH?

LISSSSBETH? CAN YOU HEAR ME?

LISBETH, CAN YOU HEAR ME?
HM
DO YOU KNOW WHERE YOU ARE?

...DRY...
CAN YOU WET LISBETH'S MOUTH, NURSE?
BETTER?
YOUR THROAT WILL BE SORE BECAUSE OF THE INTUBATION.
THAT SHOULD HEAL QUICKLY.
I'M DR. ANDERS JONASSON, LISBETH.
I'M IN CHARGE OF YOUR CARE HERE.
CAN YOU COUNT FROM 1 TO 10 FOR ME?
ONE, TWO, THREE, FOUR, FIVE...UH.
VERY GOOD. GOOD FIRST TRY. VERY PROMISING.
I DON'T KNOW HOW MUCH YOU REMEMBER. WE REMOVED A BULLET FROM YOUR BRAIN.
THAT YOU'RE CONSCIOUS ALREADY IS A GREAT SIGN.
...HAHA...

I'M SORRY, LISBETH. WHAT DID YOU SAY THEN?
WHERE ZALA?
WHERE AM I?
WHERE... IS...ZALA?
WHO IS ZALA?
OLD MAN.
AXE MAN.
AXE IN MAN.
GOOD SIGNS.
VERY GOOD.
SHE EVEN REMEMBERS AN OLD MAN WAS ADMITTED WITH HER.
NO INFORMATION, IF SHE ASKS AGAIN?
PATIENT CONFIDENTIALITY TAKES PRECEDENCE. HE GETS NO INFORMATION ABOUT HER EITHER.
MAKE SURE THE OTHER NURSES KNOW THAT.

HELP ME! PLEASE! SOMEONE! HELP ME!
THOOM THOOM

OH, HI!
HOW ARE YOU?
HAVEN'T SEEN YOU FOR AGES!
SO NICE TO SEE YOU.
YOU LOOK WELL.
BEEN BUSY, HAVE YOU?
SO NICE TO SEE YOU AGAIN.
YOU LOOK WELL.
SO NICE SO NICENICENICE.
STILL DRY?
MORE WATER?
MMMM.

I'LL TELL DR. JONASSON THAT YOU'RE AWAKE.
THE OLD MAN. AXE. WANTS TO KILL ME
WHERE IS HE?
TWO DOORS DOWN.
THANK YOU.

23 missed calls.
MALM:
B: Get 1st train home. DO IT NOW!

SJ
SJ 2000

STOCKHOLM
11:45 pm

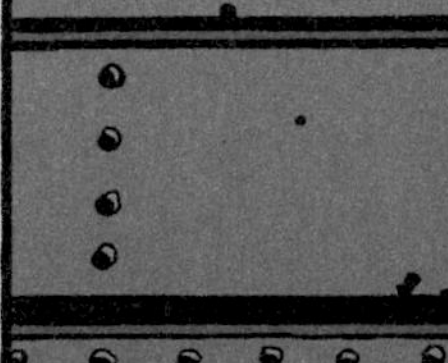
3

HI.
IS SHE OKAY?
HI, BLOMKVIST.
SHE'S AWAKE.
WON'T KNOW FOR A COUPLE OF WEEKS.

COFFEE AND SANDWICHES, PLEASE.
HAM OR CHEESE?
HAM.

SHE'S NOT MENTALLY ILL.
I THINK YOU KNOW THAT.

I DON'T KNOW ANYTHING, MR. JOURNALIST.
I THINK YOU DO, MS. POLICE OFFICER.

I THINK BUBBLE KNOWS SOMETHING SINISTER IS GOING ON, TOO.
I THINK YOU ALL KNOW.
BUT THE MANAGEMENT WON'T LET YOU PURSUE IT.

LISBETH HAS BEEN PERSECUTED SINCE SHE WAS TWELVE. YOU'VE SEEN THE 1991 PSYCHIATRIC REPORT.
BJÖRCK ***SPECIFICALLY*** TELLS DR. TELEBORIAN SHE IS A DANGER TO SÄPO AND ***MUST*** BE FOUND MENTALLY ILL AND DETAINED.
YOU ***KNOW*** THAT SHE WAS RAPED BY HER LEGAL GUARDIAN AND THAT SHE COULDN'T GO TO THE POLICE.

SHE'S BEEN LET DOWN, TIME AND ***TIME*** AGAIN.
WE CAN'T LET THAT HAPPEN THIS TIME.
LOOK, BLOMKVIST, I KNOW YOU'RE A GOOD MAN, BUT MY BOSSES--

IF YOU WANT TO TALK TO ME--***IF*** YOU WANT TO HELP HER--
YOU CAN CONTACT ME. I WILL KEEP YOUR IDENTITY A SECRET.
I ***PROTECT*** MY SOURCES.

BLOMKVIST, WE'RE ***ALL*** BEING WATCHED.
EVEN BUBBLE IS HAVING TO GO BEHIND OUR BOSSES' BACKS TO DO HIS JOB--

SET UP AN E-MAIL ACCOUNT ON HOTMAIL.
E-MAIL ME HERE.
I WILL ***NEVER MENTION YOUR NAME.***

IS THE NURSE NIEDERMANN KIDNAPPED OK?
FINE. TRAUMATIZED BUT UNHURT.
NOW HER CAR HAS COMPLETELY DISAPPEARED.
HE MUST BE SOMEWHERE.
YEAH, SOMEWHERE.
MALM
COFFEE? EGGS? CEREAL?
WHAT'S GOING ON?
ERIKA IS LEAVING MILLENNIUM.
SHE'S GOING TO SVENSKA MORGON-POSTEN AS CHIEF EDITOR.
FUCK!
GOOD FOR HER.
SHIT FOR US...
BUT GOOD FOR HER.
IT'S THE BIGGEST DAILY NEWSPAPER IN SWEDEN!

WHEN?
SHE'S LEFT ALREADY.
SHE STARTS THERE TOMORROW.
WHY DIDN'T SHE SAY?
SHE WANTED TO TELL YOU FIRST.
BUT YOU'RE NEVER THERE.
I THOUGHT SHE WANTED A BABY!
NO.
BASICALLY, SHE WANTS TO LEAVE HER BABY.
SHIT. I GOT THAT SO WRONG.
SHE SLEPT IN THE OFFICE LAST NIGHT.
ONE LAST TIME.
GO AND SEE HER, MIKEY.

THANKS FOR THAT.
WHAT HAPPENED TO YOUR JACKET, MAN?

JUST FUCKING DRIVE, MAN.

MAGGE LUNDIN?
CHARGED WITH KIDNAPPING.
HE WON'T BE COMING OUT FOR A WHILE.
LOST A BIT OF HIS FOOT TO A BULLET ANYWAY.

YOU BASTARDS REORGANIZED WHILE WE'VE BEEN INSIDE?
JUST LIKE YOU SAID: VIKTOR'S STILL THE MONEYMAN.
BENNY K GOT STEPPED UP. I'M ACTING FOR YOU AS LEADER.

BENNY *FUCKING* K? THE KID'S A FUCKING CRETIN!
I KNOW, WE'RE SHORT OF PROSPECTS. BUT THERE'S SOMETHING ELSE...

OUR GIANT BASTARD FRIEND TURNED UP--
--SAID HE WAS IN A BIT OF TROUBLE.

NIEDERMANN?!
HE'S *NOT* "IN TROUBLE." HE'S THE FUCKING REASON LUNDIN'S BEEN ARRESTED!

WELL, WE DIDN'T KNOW THAT. BENNY K TOOK HIM TO A HIDE-OUT.
WHERE?

WELL...HE TOOK HIM TO VIKTOR'S HOUSE.
BENNY TOOK HIM TO OUR MONEYMAN? YOU FUCKING ARSEHOLES!

DRIVE!
I AM DRIVING.
DRIVE FASTER.

LIGHTS ARE OUT...
CAN'T FUCKING BELIEVE YOU BROUGHT HIM HERE.
NO ONE KNOWS ABOUT VIKTOR.
WE THOUGHT HE WAS A FRIEND OF THE CLUB.
ALL OUR FUCKING MONEY'S HERE, MAN!

VIK?
VIK? ARE YOU AROUND?

VIK...?

800,000 KRONOR.
HE'S TAKEN IT ALL.
WHAT DO WE DO NOW?
PHONE THE FUCKING COPS, MAN.
WHAT ELSE ***CAN*** WE DO?

WE COULD UP THE DIAMORPHINE.
YES, DOCTOR.
NO MORE CONSCIOUS EPISODES?
NOT TODAY.
THE WOUND HEALING CLEANLY?
YES, DOCTOR.
THE PAIN WILL PROBABLY GET WORSE.
WE NEED TO MAKE SURE SHE'S ADEQUATELY MEDICATED.
YES, DOCTOR.
JUST BECAUSE SHE'S NOT CONSCIOUS DOESN'T MEAN SHE ISN'T FEELING IT.
THE GIRL WHO CAME IN WITH ME..
...SHE'S MY DAUGHTER.
OH, REALLY.

SHE WAS VERY BADLY HURT.
REALLY?
SHOT THREE TIMES.
REALLY?
...VERY WORRYING FOR A FATHER...
...HIS DAUGHTER IS LYING THERE...
...STRUGGLING FOR LIFE.
IS SHE DOING ALL RIGHT?
WE'RE NOT ALLOWED TO DISCUSS PATIENTS.
NICE TO KNOW WE'RE IN THE SAME WARD...
I DIDN'T SAY THAT.

MR. BODIN, A FEW MOMENTS OF YOUR TIME, PLEASE.
WHERE'S THAT *WHORE* POLICEWOMAN?
WE THOUGHT WE COULD GET MORE SENSE OUT OF YOU IF YOU WERE TALKING TO MEN. YOU SEEM TO HAVE A PROBLEM WITH WOMEN.
I DON'T HAVE A PROBLEM WITH WOMEN--JUST *WHORES.*
...CREEPY MAN...
I SEE.
AND I *KNOW* A WHORE WHEN I SEE ONE.
THAT'S VERY NINETEENTH CENTURY OF YOU... WHAT CAN YOU TELL ME ABOUT RONALD NIEDERMANN'S WHEREABOUTS?
NOTHING. I'M THE VICTIM HERE.
WE FOUND A LOT OF BLOOD IN THE SHALLOW GRAVE OUTSIDE YOUR HOUSE--
--LISBETH SALANDER'S BLOOD.
WE WANT TO TALK ABOUT YOUR ATTEMPTED MURDER--
I'M A HELPLESS OLD MAN WITH A DISABILITY AND HORRIFIC INJURIES, LISBETH SALANDER ATTACKED ME.
SHE TRIED TO *KILL* ME.
DON'T YOU GET IT?!
YOU SHOULD ARREST HER, NOT ME!

POLIS
POLIS
8 1960

HIS CAR: MAKE AND MODEL.
SAAB.
I WROTE THE REGISTRATION NUMBER DOWN HERE.

"AV."
MHMM MMEMH?
YES, INSPECTOR ERLANDER, A SAAB.
MHEHAMM?
OH YEAH.

WHAT COLOR IS THE SAAB?
BEIGE.
ANYTHING ELSE MISSING?
NO.

CAN'T BELIEVE WE CALLED THE COPS, MAN.
CAN'T HAVE NIEDERMANN RUNNING AROUND.
HE'S BEYOND DANGEROUS.

OH!
YOU GAVE ME A SURPRISE!
I DIDN'T HEAR YOU COME IN!
EXCUSE ME.
I REQUIRE TO SEE KARL AXEL BODIN.
THANK YOU.

WHO THE FUCK ARE YOU?
I'M YOUR BEST FRIEND.
MAYBE YOU SHOULD TELL ME YOUR NAME THEN...?
YOU DON'T NEED TO KNOW MY NAME.
DON'T BE AFRAID.
I'M NOT AFRAID.
YOU'D BE A FOOL NOT TO BE AFRAID. YOU'RE IN A BED...
YOU HAVE NO WEAPON...
YOU'RE TALKING TOO MUCH.
DO YOU KNOW WHAT THAT TELLS ME?
YOU'RE A SÄPO MESSAGE BOY.
YOU HAVE NO POWER.
IT HAS GONE VERY BADLY.
WE HAVE TO TALK ABOUT DAMAGE CONTROL.

NO, WE DON'T.
WE NEED TO TALK ABOUT WHAT YOU CAN DO FOR ME.
I'M NOT HERE TO TALK ABOUT THAT.
YOU'RE NOT QUALIFIED TO TALK ABOUT THAT. YOU'RE GOING TO CARRY MY MESSAGE TO THEM.
RONALD NIEDERMANN IS THE SCAPEGOAT. BLAME HIM FOR EVERYTHING.
HE'S GONE ANYWAY, THEY'LL NEVER FIND HIM.
SALANDER, WELL, SHE KNOWS TOO MUCH.
SHE NEEDS TO DISAPPEAR. SHE NEEDS TO BE FOUND MENTALLY INCOMPETENT.
HOSPITALIZED AGAIN, FOREVER THIS TIME. OBVIOUSLY, I KNOW YOU CAN'T KILL HER.
IF YOU COULD KILL HER--YOU COULD KILL ME.
AND YOU HAVEN'T.

HERE'S WHAT I WANT:
I WALK ON ALL CHARGES. FIX IT.
WE CAN'T DO THAT THIS TIME--
THERE'S FORENSIC EVIDENCE.
YOU'VE DONE IT BEFORE...
DO IT AGAIN.
YOU DON'T UNDERSTAND, IT'S A DIFFERENT TIME NOW.
SINCE THE END OF THE COLD WAR--OUR SECTION HAS BEEN DISBANDED.
YOU WANT THE PRESS TO HEAR?
ABOUT THE SECTION'S EXISTENCE. ALL THE SCRAPES YOU PULLED ME OUT OF?
WHO WAS INVOLVED... WHAT THEY DID...
YOU'RE THREATENING TO REVEAL THAT WE HELPED YOU BEFORE?
EVERY KINDNESS IS A WEAKNESS.
YOU'D DO WELL TO REMEMBER THAT.

THERE, THAT'S BETTER.
THERE, I'LL LEAVE YOU IN PEACE.
SEE IF YOU CAN GET SOME SLEEP.
FSSSSSSR FSSSSSSPPR
FSSSSSSR FSSSSSSPP

FSSSSSSP
FSSSSSSPPP

HIS FAKE IDENTITY IS IMPOSSIBLE TO DISPROVE.
WHAT DO YOU MEAN?
KARL AXEL BODIN WAS BORN, HE WENT TO SCHOOL...
...PASSED HIS DRIVING TEST. ALL DOCUMENTED.

THE *GIVE-AWAY* IS THAT THERE IS *JUST* ENOUGH.
NO SCHOOL PRIZES. NO TRIPS ABROAD.

BIRTH CERTIFICATE, GOVERNMENT RECORDS: THIS MEANS IT WAS AUTHORIZED ***WAY BEYOND*** SÄPO.
IT DEFINITELY DOES. IT HAS TO GO ALL THE WAY TO THE TOP.

WHO WAS THE PRIME MINISTER TWENTY-EIGHT YEARS AGO?
THORBJÖRN FÄLLDIN.

HAVE YOU GOT A POSTER?
"SWEDISH PRIME MINISTERS OF TIMES GONE BY"?

NO. I KNOW HIM.
HOW CAN *YOU* KNOW HIM?
HE LIVES NEAR MY DAD IN ÅS.
I'VE KNOWN HIM ALL MY LIFE.

WE NEED A WAY IN TO THE CASE.
A WAY TO BYPASS.
THE SECURITY SERVICES AND GOVERNMENTAL DEPARTMENTS.

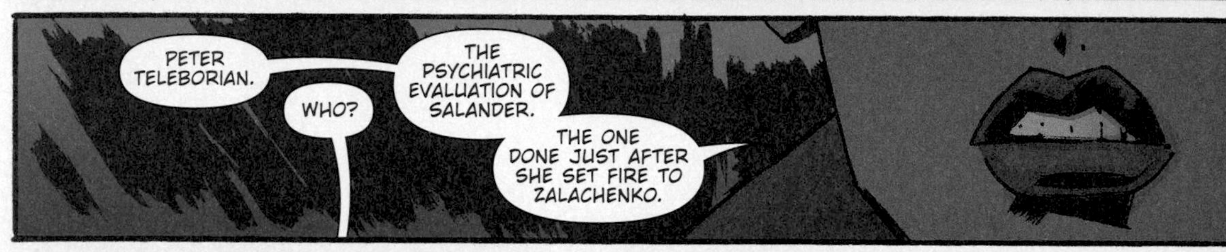
THE PSYCHIATRIC EVALUATION OF SALANDER.
THE ONE DONE JUST AFTER SHE SET FIRE TO ZALACHENKO.
WHO?
PETER TELEBORIAN.

HE'S THE PSYCHIATRIST WHO WROTE THE REPORT.

THE REPORT THAT SAID SHE WAS INSANE AND SHOULD BE HELD FOREVER.

PETER TELEBORIAN.
LET'S HAVE A LITTLE LOOK AT HIM.

-CLINTON
-WADENSJÖÖ
-ME
13

SHOP ON THE ROAD
ON SALE

FSSSSSppp
FSSSSSSppp
MR. BODIN!

OH DEAR ME, YOU SHOULDN'T BE OUT OF YOUR ROOM, MR. BODIN.
YOU MUSTN'T WALK ON THAT LEG. LET'S GET YOU BACK AND POP YOU INTO BED.
MY, MY, WHAT WERE YOU THINKING?
NOW THEN, IT'S VERY LATE.
TRY AND GET SOME SLEEP, MR. BODIN.
H

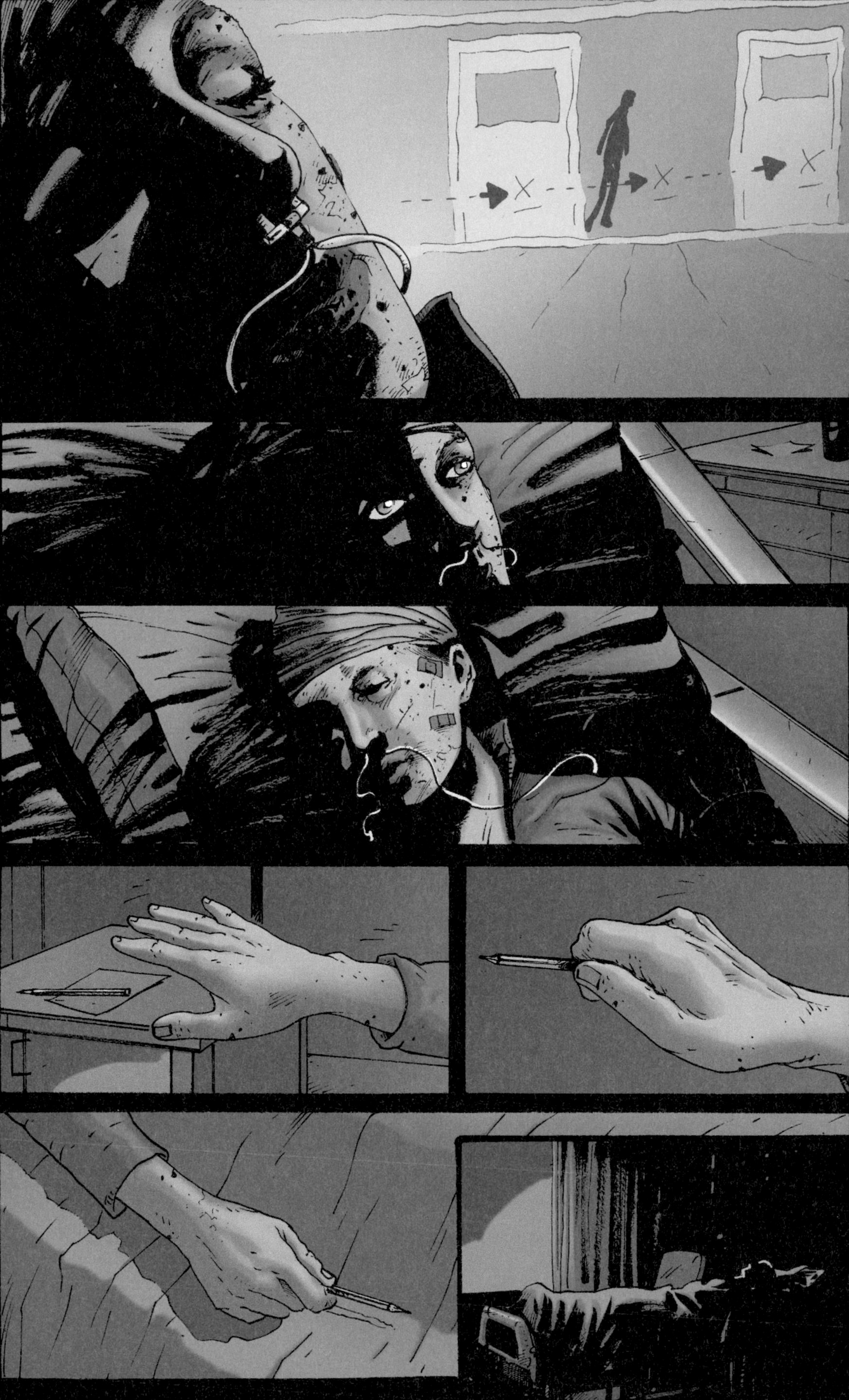

YOU'RE SAYING THEY'LL CHARGE LISBETH WITH ATTEMPTED MURDER?
THERE'S NO DOUBT THEY WILL.
BUT A CONVICTION ISN'T WHAT THEY'RE AFTER.
A CONVICTION WON'T SILENCE HER.
THE LAST THING THEY WANT IS LISBETH ALIVE, IN PRISON, AND TALKING.
YOU THINK THEY'LL ARGUE INSANITY?
THEY WILL. IT WON'T MATTER HOW THEY GET THAT FINDING.
THE 'ELEBORIAN/ ÖRCK REPORT FROM HER ONVICTION IN 991 SHOWS THEY'LL DO ANYTHING.
THAT THEY CAN DO ANYTHING.
WHO IS THEY?
THE SECURITY SERVICES.
THEY DIDN'T WANT PEOPLE TO KNOW ABOUT ZALACHENKO'S DEFECTION IN THE '80S.

BUT NOW THEY'RE DOING SOMETHING WORSE. THEY'RE COVERING THEIR OWN BACKS.
IF THIS COMES OUT... THE PUBLIC WILL KNOW *WHAT* THEY DID TO PROTECT HIM.
DETAINING SALANDER IN A PSYCHIATRIC INSTITUTE?
AND KEEPING HER THERE. THEY HAVE EVERY REASON TO DO IT AGAIN.
YOU KNOW, MIKAEL, I LOVE SALANDER LIKE A DAUGHTER.
BUT THEY CAN'T *NOT* TRY HER. THAT'S WHAT I KEEP GETTING STUCK AT...
SHE HIT A MAN IN THE FACE WITH AN AXE.
I'M NOT SUGGESTING WE STOP THEM FROM HAVING A CRIMINAL TRIAL. I'M SUGGESTING SOMETHING MUCH MORE RADICAL...
WHAT?
I'M NOT GOING TO TELL YOU ANYTHING UNTIL YOU GIVE ME YOUR ASSURANCE.
ASSURANCE OF *WHAT?*

WILL YOU DO ANYTHING TO HELP HER?
NO.
I WON'T "DO ANYTHING" TO HELP HER.
I'LL MAKE ALL MY RESOURCES AVAILABLE TO YOU, I'LL WORK NIGHT AND DAY...
...BUT I WON'T "DO ANYTHING." I'M NOT A "DO ANYTHING" SORT OF PERSON, MIKAEL.
LISBETH'S LIFE HAS BEEN PLAGUED BY THOSE WHO'D "DO ANYTHING" TO SECURE AN OUTCOME.
YOU DON'T NEED TO TELL ME OFF, DRAGAN.
I WON'T BREAK HER OUT OR ANYTHING LIKE THAT.
CALM DOWN:
WE JUST NEED YOUR CONNECTIONS, THAT'S ALL.
WE NEED TO MAKE THIS BIGGER THAN A CRIMINAL TRIAL.
AND IT STARTS WITH MY BIG SISTER.

EMERGENCY
NURSE?
NURSE, WHAT IS THIS DOING HERE?
IT SHOULDN'T BE THERE.
I'M SORRY DOCTOR,
I DON'T KNOW HOW IT GOT THERE.
IT MUST HAVE ROLLED THERE.
PLEASE BE MORE CAREFUL.

DENNIS PUB
dennis pub
DID YOU THINK ABOUT IT?
I DID.
WILL YOU DO IT?
IF LISBETH REFUSES TO COOPERATE WITH THE STRATEGY...
...WHICH SOUNDS PRETTY LIKELY, FROM WHAT YOU'VE TOLD ME ABOUT HER.
IT WON'T WORK.
BUT IF SHE DOES?
THERE'S AN OUTSIDE CHANCE THAT IT *MIGHT* WORK.

I DON'T KNOW IF IT'S FAIR TO RISK HER FREEDOM.
IF WE DON'T, SHE'LL GET A PSYCHIATRIC DISPOSAL.
ARE YOU SURE THAT'S WRONG?
MIKEY, SHE SOUNDS PRETTY MESSED UP.
YES.
SHE IS.
YOU'D BE MESSED UP, TOO, IF THE STATE HAD CONSPIRED TO SHUT YOU UP SINCE THE AGE OF TWELVE.
WILL YOU?
FOR ***FUCKSAKE***, MIKEY! YOU KNEW I WOULD WHEN YOU ASKED ME.
THANKS, ANNIKA.
DON'T THANK ME YET. SHE MIGHT NOT COOPERATE.
STILL, YOU'RE HER ONLY CHANCE.

...REPRESENTING LISBETH SALANDER.
BUT I KNOW YOUR WORK, MS. GIANNI.
YOU'RE A CIVIL RIGHTS LAWYER, *NOT* A CRIMINAL LAWYER.
YOU'RE DOING A GOOD JOB OF SOUNDING LIKE A CRIMINAL LAWYER.
YOU *MAY* ASK HER ABOUT RONALD NIEDERMANN'S WHEREABOUTS AND THE EVENTS AT THE GOSSEBERGA FARM.
YOU CANNOT ASK HER ABOUT ANYTHING ELSE PERTAINING TO THE WIDER CASE AGAINST HER.
IS THAT CLEAR, INSPECTOR ERLANDER?
FOR THE PURPOSES OF THIS CASE, I AM ONE.
VERY GOOD.

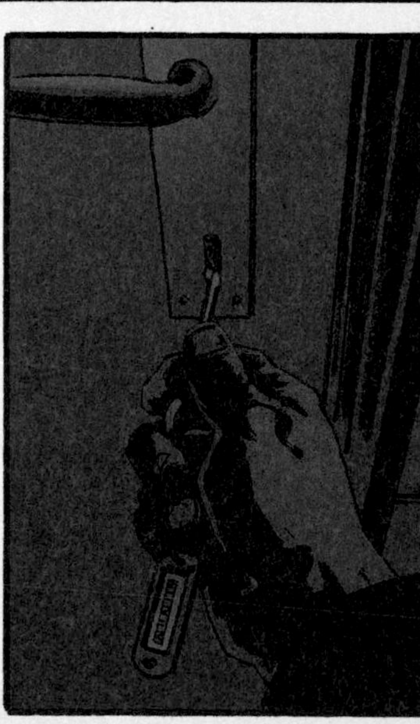

MR. EVERT GULLBERG!
WHAT AN HONOR FOR US!
TO BE LED BY THE LEGEND HIMSELF!
STOP TALKING NOW.

I'M SORRY IF I HAVE OFFENDED YOU, SIR.
TIMES MAY HAVE CHANGED, WADENSJÖÖ.
BUT TELLING A SECRET AGENT THEY ARE "A LEGEND" IS ***STILL*** IMPLICITLY INSULTING.
EVEN IF THE COLD WAR IS OVER.

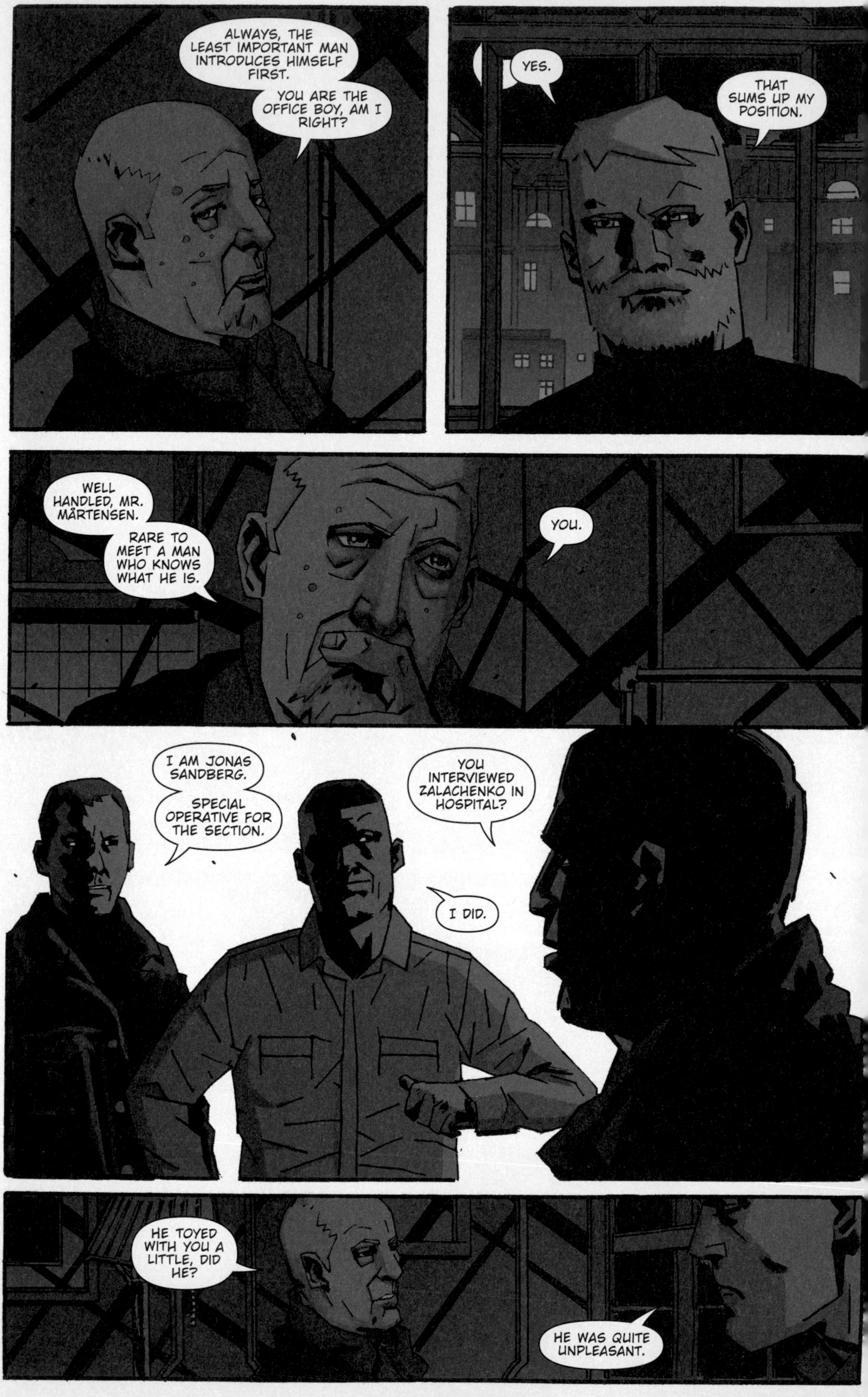

ALWAYS, THE LEAST IMPORTANT MAN INTRODUCES HIMSELF FIRST.
YOU ARE THE OFFICE BOY, AM I RIGHT?

YES.
THAT SUMS UP MY POSITION.

WELL HANDLED, MR. MÅRTENSEN.

RARE TO MEET A MAN WHO KNOWS WHAT HE IS.

YOU.

I AM JONAS SANDBERG.

SPECIAL OPERATIVE FOR THE SECTION.

YOU INTERVIEWED ZALACHENKO IN HOSPITAL?

I DID.

HE TOYED WITH YOU A LITTLE, DID HE?
HE WAS QUITE UNPLEASANT.

HE SAW THAT YOU ARE VAIN AND PLAYED ON THAT.
HE TOLD YOU THAT YOU WERE UNIMPORTANT, DID HE?
HE IMPLIED IT.
YOU'RE **NOT.** NONE OF YOU ARE.
BUT HE KNEW YOU WOULD CARE... HE'S VERY SKILLED.
YOU KNOW WHO I AM.
WADENSJÖÖ, YOU MAY BE HEAD OF THE SECTION NOW.
BUT YOUR POSITION IS HONORARY.
YOU ARE NOT FIT TO RUN AN OPERATION AGAINST SOMEONE LIKE ZALACHENKO.
NONE OF YOU ARE.
I'M TAKING OVER THIS OPERATION FORTHWITH.

CAN YOU GIVE ME THE DAYS OF THE WEEK, LISBETH?
MONDAY, TUESDAY, WEDNESDAY, THURSDAY, FRIDAY SATURDAY, SUNDAY.
GOOD. COUNTING?
1,2,3, 4,5,6,7,8, ETC.
"ETC."?
YOU'RE A BRAIN SURGEON.
I'M WORKING UNDER THE ASSUMPTION THAT YOU KNOW THE REST.
THAT IS A CORRECT ASSUMPTION. HEADACHES?
YES.
HOW OFTEN?
INCESSANT.
WE'LL UP THE PAINKILLERS.
HE'S WALKING NOW?
WHO?
ZALACHENKO. MY FATHER.

WHY WOULD YOU THINK THAT?
HE'S ON CRUTCHES BUT HE'S MOBILE.
IT WOULD BE BAD FOR YOU TO TRY TO RUSH YOUR RECOVERY, LISBETH.
YOU HAVE SUFFERED A TRAUMATIC INJURY TO THE BRAIN.
YOU WILL HAVE TO BE PATIENT.
CAN I HAVE SOME CIGARETTES?
NO.
CAN I HAVE A GUN?
ALSO: NO.
I'M GOING TO GET A NICOTINE PATCH FOR YOU.
WHAT STRENGTH DO YOU NEED?
STRONG AS THEY MAKE THEM...

THERE IS ONE, AND ONLY ONE, PIECE OF DOCUMENTATION TYING US TO THE INCARCERATION OF LISBETH SALANDER.

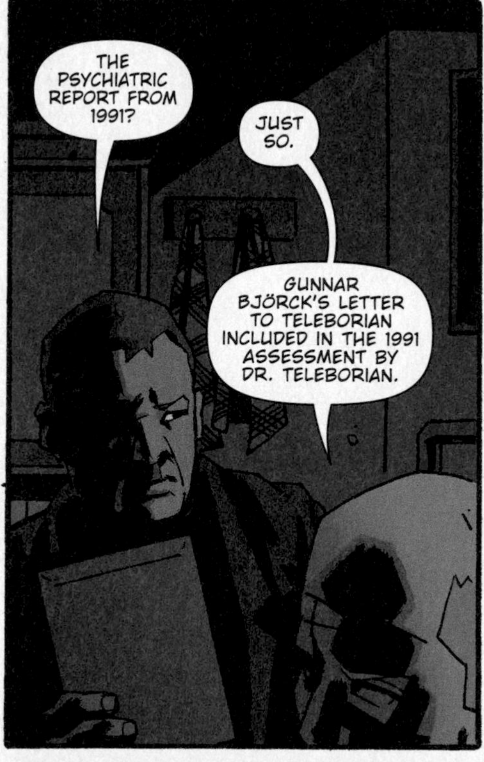

THE PSYCHIATRIC REPORT FROM 1991?
JUST SO.
GUNNAR BJÖRCK'S LETTER TO TELEBORIAN INCLUDED IN THE 1991 ASSESSMENT BY DR. TELEBORIAN.

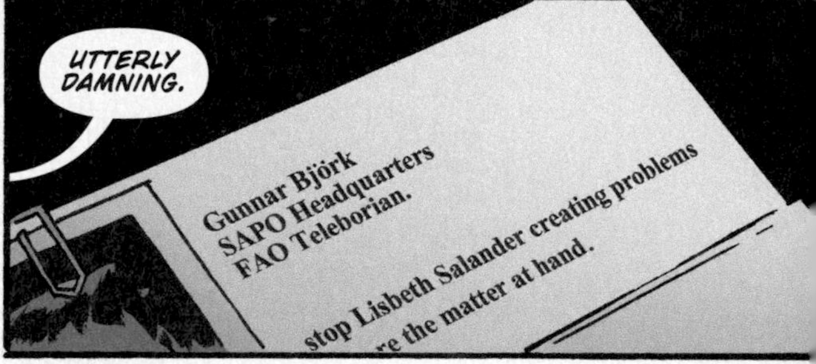

UTTERLY DAMNING.
Gunnar Björk
SAPO Headquarters
FAO Teleborian.
stop Lisbeth Salander creating problems
re the matter at hand.

TRACE EVERY SINGLE COPY.
GET THEM BACK.

DOCUMENTATION ASIDE, WE HAVE ONE OTHER PROBLEM.
AND IT'S *BIG*.

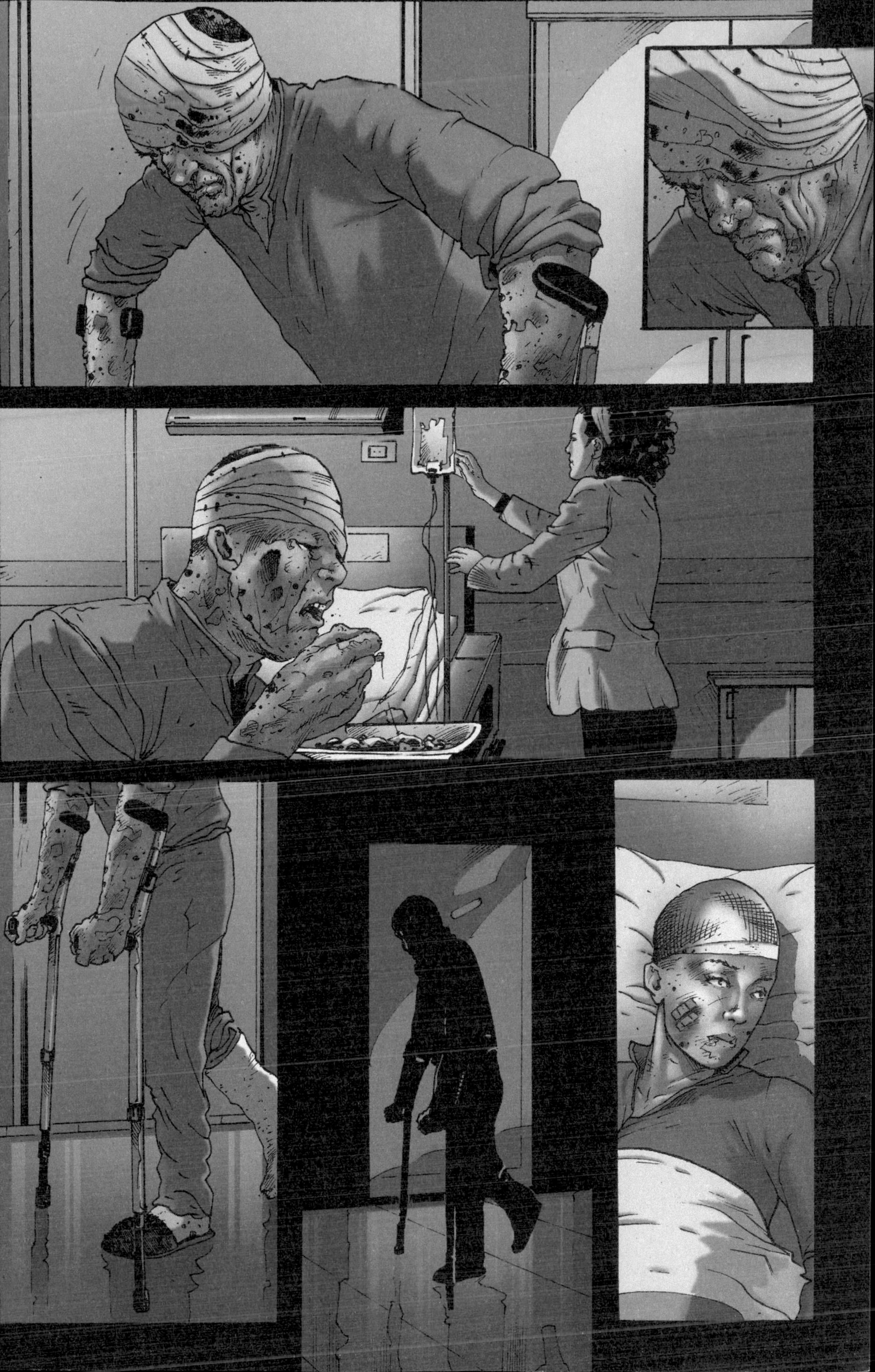

1

ONE LAST MANEUVER, FREDRIK.
EVERT, I CAN'T DO IT.
I'M ON DIALYSIS EVERY SECOND DAY.
ALL DAY.

THEY'RE GOOD OPERATIVES, FREDRIK.
BUT THEY HAVE NO STEEL.
THEY AREN'T PREPARED FOR WHAT WILL HAPPEN.
AFTERWARDS.

FSSSP
FSSSSSSP
OH REALLY, NOT AGAIN.
COME ON. BACK YOU GO!
FSSSSSSP

LISBETH SALANDER.
CAN WE ASK YOU SOME QUESTIONS?
WE HAVE BEEN ADVISED THAT ANNIKA GIANNI IS REPRESENTING YOU.
IS THAT CORRECT?
WE HAVEN'T MET YET.
SHE CAME TO SEE ME.
SHE SAYS I MAY ASK ABOUT THE WHEREABOUTS OF RONALD NIEDERMANN BUT NOTHING ELSE.
NIEDERMANN HAS LEFT THE COUNTRY.
ZALACHENKO TOLD ME AT THE FARM.
IT WAS SET UP BEFORE HE EVEN SHOT ME.
THE ROUTE, HIDING PLACES, AND FUNDS WERE ALL IN PLACE.
ZALA SAID NO ONE WOULD FIND HIM.

DID HE MENTION WHICH COUNTRY?
NO.
HE'S NOT AN IDIOT.
...HE'S A SHIT.
BUT NOT AN IDIOT.
HE SAYS YOU TRIED TO KILL HIM.
DID YOU FIND A GRAVE FULL OF MY BLOOD?
WE DID.
BLEEDING INTO AN OPEN GRAVE. DOES THAT SEEM LIKE A WAY TO KILL SOMEONE?
I SUPPOSE... MOST ASSASSINS WOULD TRY SOMETHING ELSE.

FSSSSSSppp
FSSSSSp
MEEP
MEEP
MEEP
MEEP
MEEP
MEEP
OH NOW, COME ON, MR. BODIN. JUST RING THE BELL.
YOU MUSTN'T COME OUT HER LOOKING FOR L BACK TO BED WITH YOU.
MEEP
MEEP
MEEP

OF COURSE...
ALWAYS SOMETHING...
...ADDRESSES.
OF JUSTICE
ROSENBAD 4
SE-103 33
STOCKHOLM

IT DOESN'T MAKE SENSE.
HOW COULD THEY INCARCERATE HER FROM THE AGE OF TWELVE?
WITHOUT ANYONE OBJECTING OR BREAKING RANKS?
I'VE READ ALL OF THESE, TOO, MIKEY.
AND YOU'RE RIGHT: THE POWER STRUCTURE OF SÄPO MEANS THAT THEY ALL KNEW.
BUT SÄPO OPERATIVES AREN'T AMORAL.
THEY DON'T JOIN THE SECURITY SERVICES TO PERSECUTE CHILDREN AND PROTECT CRIMINALS.
SOMEONE WOULD HAVE OBJECTED.
SO IT CAN'T HAVE BEEN DONE BY SÄPO BUT IT USES ALL THEIR RESOURCES.
A SECRET SUB-COMMITTEE?
HAND-PICKED BY A SENIOR SÄPO OVERLORD.
AND THEY WOULD HAVE BEEN GIVEN THE JOB.

THEY'D HAVE BEEN HANDLING THIS OPERATION FOR YEARS.
COVERING UP FOR ZALA, ORDERING SALANDER'S DETENTION, GETTING RID OF ANYONE.
THEY WOULD'VE RETIRED BY NOW, SURELY?
HALF OF THEM WOULD BE DEAD.
THE DEAD ONES DON'T WORRY ME BUT THE LIVING TERRIFY ME...
THESE ARE SCARY PEOPLE. THESE ARE COLD WAR OPERATIVES.
WHEN THIS COMES OUT, THEIR LIFE'S WORK'LL BE ON THE LINE.
"THE PAST JUDGED THROUGH THE LENS OF THE PRESENT." COLD WAR OPS JUDGED BY THE SANCTIMONIOUS NOW.
THEY'LL BE FRANTIC. A LOT OF THEM ARE VERY HARDENED.
VIOLENT... FERAL...
CORTEZ: I THINK WE'RE GOING TO NEED A BIGGER BOAT.
WE DON'T NEED A BOAT, MIKEY, WE NEED A NUCLEAR SUB.

YOU HAVE THE LETTERS WRITTEN?
YES.
ALL ELEVEN?
YES, FREDERIK.
PHOTOCOPIED IN CASE THEY GET LOST?
I WILL DO THAT ON MY WAY TO THE POST OFFICE.
AND FILE THEM CAREFULLY.
SO THEY CAN BE FOUND.
OF COURSE.
A SMALL PROBLEM FOR AFTERWARDS:
THE INVESTIGATION INTO THE GOSSEBERGA FARM INCIDENT WILL CONTINUE.
WE NEED TO ENSURE ITS CONTAINMENT.
HANS FASTE.
VERY CLEVER.
I KNEW YOU'D THINK OF SOMETHING.

TYPING OFFICE
copies!
copies!
8am - 7pm
TYPING CENTER
fast&self!

THANK YOU, NURSE.
NO PROBLEM, MR. PALMGREN. I'LL BE JUST OUTSIDE.
CALL ME WHEN YOU HAVE FINISHED.
WHY ARE WE ALL HERE?
ME, TOO.
MIKEY ASKED ME TO COME.
I'M GUESSING WE ARE ALL INVOLVED WITH A CERTAIN CASE.
I'M NOT THAT BUSY ANYWAY.
THANKS FOR COMING, EVERYONE.
THANKS FOR INVITING THESE PEOPLE INTO MY OFFICE.
ONLY SAFE PLACE FOR ALL OF US TO MEET.
LISBETH SALANDER.
THAT IS WHO WE ALL HAVE IN COMMON.
AND UNTIL TODAY I HAD NO IDEA WHAT SHE WAS UP AGAINST.
WHAT ARE YOU TALKING ABOUT?
LISBETH'S LIFE IS NOT A SERIES OF MISHAPS AND MISFORTUNES.
YES, IT IS.

NO, IT ISN'T, HOLGER.
IT LOOKS LIKE THAT.
BUT IT *ISN'T.*
LISBETH HAS BEEN A COLD WAR FOOTBALL. THE SECURITY SERVICES HAVE BEEN COVERING UP.
AND IN THE NEXT FEW MONTHS *EVERYONE* HERE NEEDS TO APPRECIATE WHAT WE'RE UP AGAINST.
WE'RE THE DON QUIXOTES:
FIGHTING A CAUSE LOST *LONG* AGO.
NO, IT WASN'T.
WE'RE ALL PLEDGED TO HER IN ONE WAY OR ANOTHER AND WE NEED TO WATCH OUT FOR ONE ANOTHER.
THAT'S WRONG.
IS NO ONE GOING TO LISTEN TO ME?
SORRY, HOLGER.
WE ALL KNOW HER.
WE ALL KNOW WHAT SHE'S CAPABLE OF...
IF WE CAN BE AS STOIC AS SHE IS...AS IMMUNE TO HARDSHIP AND RIDICULE...
AND HALF AS *SMART*, WE MIGHT JUST HAVE A CHANCE OF SAVING HER.

I'M VISITING MY GRANNY.
LUCKY YOU.
GET WELL SOON
SHE'S GOT CHOCOLATES.
SHE GIVES ME THEM BECAUSE SHE DOESN'T FEEL HUNGRY.
LUCKY YOU.
INTENSIVE CARE UNIT

...I'M HER LAWYER...
I'M SORRY TO DO THIS, BUT SECURITY IS VERY TIGHT JUST NOW.
PLEASE, JUST THROUGH THERE.
THANKS, NURSE.
WE'RE BEING VERY CAREFUL.
AS YOU SHOULD BE.
GOOD DAY, NURSE.
I'M HERE TO VISIT KARL AXEL BODIN.
I'M SO SORRY, SIR. I'M AFRAID MR. BODIN IS NOT ALLOWED VISITORS.

OH, HE'S A VERY OLD FRIEND. I'VE COME ALL THIS WAY.
I BOUGHT THESE FLOWERS...
I'M SO SORRY.
WOULD YOU GIVE THEM TO HIM?

MR. BODIN, SOME LOVELY FLOWERS FOR YOU.
FROM A FRIEND.
FLOWERS?
I DON'T WANT FLOWERS. THOSE ONES STINK.
YOU DON'T LIKE THEM?
GET THEM OUT OF HERE...
OR I'LL FUCKING SPEW.
WELL, I'LL PUT THEM ON THE NURSES' STATION.
GIVE THE PLACE A NICE SMELL.
WHAT?!

HELLO, LISBETH.
DO YOU KNOW WHO I AM?
...BLOMKVIST...
YOU LOOK LIKE HIM.
I DON'T KNOW IF THAT'S GOOD OR BAD.
LISBETH, WHILE YOU WERE UNCONSCIOUS. I HAVE BEEN ACTING AS YOUR LAWYER.
I UNDERSTAND THAT YOU HAVE A HABIT OF SECRECY. I UNDERSTAND A LITTLE ABOUT WHY.
I'M NOT HERE TO PRY INTO YOUR AFFAIRS.
YOU MAY NOT WANT ME AS YOUR LAWYER BUT THIS WILL BE AN EXTREMELY COMPLEX LEGAL CASE.
YOU CAN DO WITH ALL THE HELP YOU CAN GET. I CAN ADVISE YOU.
DON'T NEED ADVICE.
NEED A PASSPORT.

HELLO.
I THOUGHT YOU'D BE DEAD BY NOW.
NEARLY, BUT NOT QUITE.
ZALACHENKO, I'M STARTING TO THINK YOU'RE IMMORTAL.
SO AM I.
WE NEED TO SORT THIS OUT.
I'M GLAD I'M FINALLY TALKING TO A BOSS.
THAT'S WHY I'M HERE. I'M HERE TO FIND OUT WHAT YOU WANT.
WELL, I DON'T M--
BLAM

BLAM

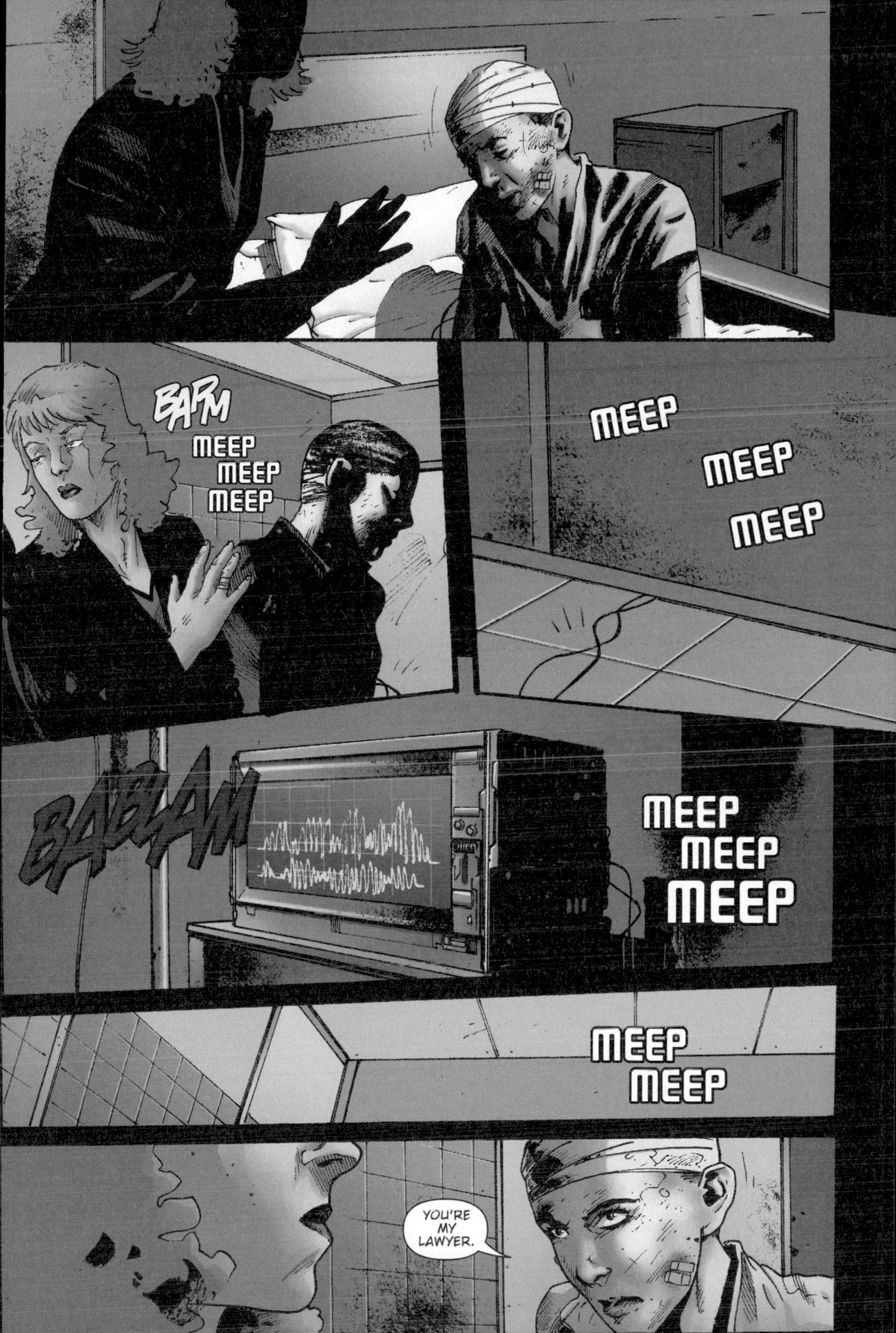
BARM
MEEP
MEEP
MEEP
MEEP
MEEP
MEEP
BABLAM
MEEP
MEEP
MEEP
MEEP
MEEP
YOU'RE MY LAWYER.

HE'S BEEN DRIVING A BEIGE SAAB FOR TWO DAYS.
AND NO ONE'S SEEN HIM OR THE CAR.
MY GUESS WOULD BE GERMANY.
SALANDER SAID HE HAD MONEY. THAT IT WAS ALL SET UP BEFORE HE EVEN LEFT.
TOO LATE NOW.
WE SHOULD HAVE PUSHED KARL AXEL BODIN.
ONE OF THE BENEFITS OF ATTEMPTING SUICIDE IN HOSPITAL...
THEY GOT THE BULLET OUT.
IF GULLBERG SURVIVES THE COMA...
PEOPLE MIGHT START *PRAYING* TO HIM.
WHO THE HELL IS EVERT GULLBERG ANYWAY?
JUST SOME CRAZY RETIRED TAX LAWYER.
WITH A GRUDGE.

HOW DID THEY KNOW HE HAD A GRUDGE?
HE HAD WRITTEN LETTERS THREATENING BODIN.
...TO THE MINISTRY OF JUSTICE.
DON'T SUPPOSE BODIN KNEW A LOT OF TAX LAWYERS.
HOW DID GULLBERG KNOW HIM?
FROM THE NEWSPAPER AND TV REPORTS ABOUT THE FARM.
THAT'S WHAT THEY SAID ANYWAY.
WHO'S "THEY"?
SÄPO.
SÄPO?
YEAH. HELL OF A THING, ISN'T IT?
NOT EXACTLY KNOWN FOR SHARING INFORMATION...
BUT THEY JUST *SPONTANEOUSLY* PHONED THE INVESTIGATION.
TO TELL US THAT HE'D WRITTEN THREATENING LETTERS?

THIS WAS THE PLAN?!
TO MURDER ZALA AND KILL HIMSELF?
HOW IS THAT "CLEANING UP"?
LIKE ALL YOUR GENERATION YOU'RE A FOOL, WADENSJÖÖ.
YOU BENEFIT FROM THE PEACE WE FOUGHT FOR, THEN FLATTER YOURSELF THAT YOU'RE BETTER THAN US.
WE WERE FORCED TO DO THINGS THAT SHAMED US. THEY WERE FORCED TO DO DEMEANING, BELITTLING THINGS.
THE PRESENT PEACE IS BUILT ON THESE ACTIONS.
WE WERE ELITE COLD WAR WARRIORS.
YOU ARE OUR SPOILED CHILDREN.
YOUR PRIVILEGE DEPENDS ON OUR BEING INVISIBLE.
GULLBERG UNDERSTOOD THIS. HE KNEW WE NEEDED TO DISAPPEAR FROM HISTORY.

BUT HE SHOULD HAVE CLEARED IT WITH ME!
I'M THE HEAD OF THIS UNIT
YOU'RE THE HEAD OF NOTHING.
YOU WERE PROMOTED TO LEAD A REDUNDANT UNIT.
WHAT DOES THAT TELL ME?
THAT YOU BELIEVE IT WAS A PROMOTION SPEAKS VOLUMES.
CALL THE NURSE AND THEN GET OUT.
MY BLOOD PRESSURE IS DROPPING AND I'VE GOT WORK TO DO.
"WORK"?
WHAT SORT OF WORK?

SAHLGRENSKA HOSPITAL TODAY.
NAMED AS KARL AXEL BODIN AND EVERT GULLBERG.
HOLY FUCK!
--ONE PRONOUNCED DEAD AT THE SCENE.
HURK--!

I GET IT!
I GET IT!
I WON'T SAY A WORD TO ANYONE!
--A SERIES OF THREATENING LETTERS FROM MR. GULLBERG-
I DON'T KNOW ANYONE.
I DON'T RECOGNIZE NAMES.
I KNOW NOTHING.
PROMISE?
I PROMISE!
CROSS YOUR HEART AND HOPE TO DIE?
CROSS MY HEART...?
AND HOPE TO DIE?

DON'T JUST STAND AROUND, FALUN.
HAVE YOU PUT THEM IN?
YUP.
WHAT'S THE BOOK?
OH, I THOUGHT IT WAS ABOUT SOMETHING...
...BUT IT WAS ABOUT SOMETHING ELSE.
Pornography and Civil Rights: A New Day for Woman's Equality
by Catherine McKinnon
THE WOMAN LAWYER.
WE'VE GOT HER PHONING SOMEONE RIGHT NOW.

OH NO, POOR YOU, SUZANNE.
OH GOD, REALLY?
YOUR POOR MUM...
PUB
WHAT DID THE RESULTS SAY?
NOT EVEN CHEMO?
THAT'S AWFUL...
SUZANNE, I'M COMING OVER.
NO, I'M COMING OVER.
SURE.

NO, JUST MY BRIEFCASE.
NO, NO AMBULANCE, I'M OKAY.
THEY HIT ME BUT THEY ONLY TOOK MY BRIEFCASE.
NO, THEY DIDN'T TAKE MY PHONE OR WALLET.
NO, I DON'T KNOW WHY...

I MEAN, HE'S A NUT CASE.
PLAINLY WORKING ON HIS OWN.
THERE'S ABSOLUTELY NO DOUBT ABOUT IT.
AN ANGRY LONER...?
PROBABLY WROTE THEM ON A GRASSY KNOLL.
WELL, I DON'T KNOW WHERE HE WROTE THEM BUT HE CLEARLY HATED KARL AXEL BODIN WITH A PASSION.
AND WENT THERE TO KILL HIM.
HE WAS A TAX LAWYER.
WORKED QUIETLY IN A ONE-MAN FIRM.
NEVER MARRIED, OR DID ANYTHING APART FROM WORK.
BUT THAT'S ALL WE KNOW NOW.
WE'LL BE INVESTIGATING HIS BACKGROUND--
NO. YOU WON'T.
WHY NOT?
THE INVESTIGATION IS TOO SPRAWLING.
WE'RE HAVING TO SPLIT IT INTO SECTIONS.
YOU WILL BE INVESTIGATING THE WAREHOUSE FIRE.
AND CONDUCTING THE SEARCH FOR RONALD NEIDERMANN.

HANS FASTE WILL BE CONTINUING WITH THE SALANDER INVESTIGATION.
I'M SURE YOU'LL AGREE--
NO!
I BEG YOUR PARDON?
THE MAN'S AN IDIOT. HE'S A BUFFOON.
HE'S NOT CAPABLE--
THAT IS NOT FOR YOU TO SAY, BUBLANSKI.
WE HAVE A CERTAIN NUMBER OF PERSONNEL. WE HAVE TO USE YOU *ALL*.
AND SINCE THE LISBETH SALANDER CASE IS SLOWING DOWN AS WE'RE BUILDING OUR CASE AGAINST HER...
...THERE REALLY ISN'T THAT MUCH TO DO.
BUT I'LL NEED CERTAIN PAPERS BACK FROM YOU, SONJA.
LIKE WHAT?
THE 1991 DR. TELEBORIAN PSYCHIATRIC REPORT.
I NEED THAT *QUITE* URGENTLY.

THEY FOUND IT AROUND THE CORNER.
NOTHING TAKEN BUT THE 1991 REPORT BY DR. TELEBORIAN.
THEY BROKE INTO MY HOUSE AND TOOK MINE, TOO.
NOW WE DON'T HAVE ANY COPIES LEFT.
I TOLD YOU WE SHOULD HAVE PRINTED IT, MIKEY.
YOU MUST HAVE BEEN SCARED, ANNIKA.
YOU KNOW ME, MIKEY.
I'M A TOUGH OLD SOD.
I GOT A FRIGHT WHEN THEY DREW UP IN THE CAR, THOUGH.
AFTER WHAT HAPPENED AT THE HOSPITAL...
...I THOUGHT THEY WERE GOING TO SHOOT ME.
WHO KNEW YOU'D BE THERE?
WHAT?
WHO KNEW YOU'D BE AT SUZANNE'S HOUSE?
NO ONE.
I'D JUST DECIDED TO GO THERE.
HER MUM HAS CANCER AND SHE'D JUST PHONED ME.

SHE PHONED YOU?
YES, SHE'D JUST PHONED ME.
MAYBE YOU CALLED HOME, TOLD YOUR HUSBAND?
NO.
WHEN I PHONED THE POLICE TO REPORT THE MUGGING--
--MY MOBILE WAS STILL WARM FROM TALKING TO HER.
OH, WELL.
THESE THINGS HAPPEN!
SURE DO!
I KNOW WHAT WOULD CHEER YOU UP!
A NICE BIG CUP OF COFFEE!
THEY'RE TAPPING YOUR PHONE...
THEY'LL BE TAPPING OUR OFFICE TOO.
AND OUR EMAILS.
WE NEED PAY-AS-YOU-GO PHONES FOR EVERYONE.
AND AD HOC EMAIL ACCOUNTS.
MIKEY, IF THEY'VE GOT YOURS AND MINE...
THAT MEANS THEY'VE GOT ALL THE COPIES OF THE 1991 PSYCHIATRIC REPORT.
NO, THEY DON'T. I'VE GOT SOME COPIES HIDDEN AWAY.
BUT WHAT'S GREAT IS THIS: THEY THINK THEY DO.

IT'S GREAT, LISBETH.
BLOOD PRESSURE, HEART RATE, EVERYTHING.
YOUR FITNESS HAS MADE A HUGE DIFFERENCE TO YOUR RECOVERY FROM THE SURGERY.
AND THE SHOOTING INCIDENT.
YOU BEEN HAVING NIGHTMARES OR ANYTHING...?
NO.
BUT I HAD A HAPPY DREAM ABOUT IT.
A HAPPY DREAM?
I DREAMED MY FATHER WAS DEAD.
I TRIED TO SAVE HIM.
IT'S MY JOB TO STOP PEOPLE FROM DYING.
EVEN ARSEHOLES?
IT'S NOT MY JOB TO JUDGE.
HIS BODY HAS BEEN MOVED TO A DIFFERENT HOSPITAL.
I FELT IT WAS BOTHERING YOU...
HIM BEING HERE.

DIDN'T BOTHER ME...
REALLY?
BEING SHOT AT WOULD BOTHER ME.
YOU'RE DOING SO WELL.
WE'LL HAVE TO RELEASE YOU SOON.
YOU KNOW THAT, DON'T YOU?
YES.
WHEN YOU'RE RELEASED, DO YOU KNOW WHERE YOU'RE GOING?
HAS YOUR LAWYER EXPLAINED IT TO YOU?
I'M GOING INTO POLICE CUSTODY.
TO FACE THE CHARGES AGAINST ME.
YOU OKAY ABOUT THAT?
DOESN'T MATTER HOW I AM ABOUT IT.
IT'S WHAT IS GOING TO HAPPEN.
CAN I HAVE MORE NICOTINE PATCHES?
NO, YOU'RE ALREADY ON THE HIGHEST DOSE.
HIGHEST DOSE FOR WHAT? MICE?

SVENSKA MORGON-POSTEN
SLIGHTLY BIGGER STAFF THAN YOU MAY BE USED TO...
WE HAVE FIFTEEN INCLUDING ADMIN STAFF.
WELL, WE'VE GOT EIGHTY REPORTERS AND NINETY ADMIN STAFF.
I'VE JUST STARTED AS DEPUTY EDITOR MYSELF, COMING FROM A FULL STAFF OF FORTY.
A BIT INTIMIDATING...
I'LL BE FINE.
ANYWAY, THE OUTGOING EDITOR WILL BE HERE WITH ME FOR THE FIRST MONTH.

WELCOME TO THIS ROTTING CORPSE, MY DEAR.
WE'RE IN THE BOWELS, HERE.
INTOXICATING SMELL, NO?
HOW IS IT ROTTING?
THIS IS THE END OF DAYS FOR PRINT JOURNALISM.
WE'VE GOT HALF THE STAFF WE HAD IN THE 1960s, AND CIRCULATION CONTINUES TO DROP THROUGH THE FLOOR.
IT'S INEVITABLE.
IT'S THE INTERNET AGE, MY DEAR.
THAT'S BULLSHIT.
AT MILLENNIUM OUR CIRCULATION HAS INCREASED BY A FACTOR OF NINE.
OF COURSE IT HAS, DEAR--
YOU'RE STARTING FROM A VERY SMALL BASE LINE.
CALL ME "DEAR" AGAIN AND I'LL PUNCH YOU.
MAYBE YOUR CIRCULATION WOULD HAVE BEEN BETTER IF YOU LAID OFF SOMEONE OTHER THAN JOURNALISTS.

WHO WOULD YOU LAY OFF?
THE STAFF SELLING ADVERTISING?
THEY GENERATE REVENUE, WHICH PAYS THE WAGES.
OR THE ADMIN STAFF?
AND HAVE HIGHLY TRAINED JOURNALISTS DOING FILING?
MY STRATEGY IS PRODUCE A BETTER PAPER THAT PEOPLE WANT TO BUY.
I ABSOLUTELY HATE YOU.
I GET THAT A LOT.
IT'S NOT MY PROBLEM ANYMORE.
I'M LOOKING FORWARD TO A LONG RETIREMENT NURSING MY HEART CONDITION.
BUT I'M SURE THE CHAIRMAN OF THE BOARD WILL *LOVE* YOUR BUSINESS PLAN.
HE'S EXPECTING US NOW.
ERIKA, WELCOME TO MORGON-POSTEN.
MAGNUS BORGSJÖ...
...LOVELY TO SEE YOU AGAIN.
I'M AFRAID YOU JOIN US AT A TIME OF FINANCIAL CRISIS.
WE NEED A PLAN--
CUT CAKES FOR SENIOR MANAGEMENT?
I'M NOT JOKING, ERIKA.
NEITHER AM I, MAGNUS.

THERE HE IS.
THE CAR OWNER'S NAME IS MÅRTENSSON, A POLICE OFFICER--
WHAT?
OH, NO, HANG ON, NO, NOW HAS A PRIVATE BUSINESS.
POLICE-TO-PRIVATE BUSINESS:
THAT'S THE USUAL ROUTE TO SECURITY SERVICES.
HAS TO BE. GOT A GOOD PICTURE OF THEM...
...WE CAN USE THAT LATER.

SEE YOU UP THERE, MIKEY.
HEY, THANKS FOR COMING.
CAN I GET YOU COFFEE?
IT'S A ONE-OFF FACT-GATHERING ASSIGNMENT.
BUT YOU CAN'T MENTION IT TO ANYONE.
YEAH?
FINE. YOU WANT A FLOOR PLAN?
AND A MAP OF EXITS AND ENTRANCES, TOO.
I'LL HAVE TO GET BLUE-PRINTS OF THE BUILDING.
THAT MIGHT COST.
WHAT-EVER YOU NEED.
BUT I NEED ALL THE PERSONNEL WHO WORK THERE, TOO.
AND THEIR BACKGROUND, TOO?
IF POSSIBLE.
SHOULDN'T BE A PROBLEM.
"HOSPITALS CENTRALIZE ALL OF THEIR PERSONNEL RECORDS.
"DON'T SEE WHY GOTHENBURG WOULD BE ANY DIFFERENT."

B.S., AS YOU SAY, MY DEAR.
TOTAL B.S., MY DEAR.
HIS PERSONAL VIEWS ARE ALL OVER IT.
IT'S GOOD JOURNALISM AND BAD STYLE.
HOLM WON'T BE PLEASED.
HE THINKS HIS POSITION IS NEUTRAL.
I'VE BEEN HERE THREE DAYS.
AND I HAVEN'T NOTICED HIM BEING PLEASED ABOUT ANYTHING.
WE'RE NOT EMPLOYING HIM FOR HIS SOCIAL CHARM...
...LUCKILY.
AH, LUNCHEON!
THANKS, MS. BERGER.
DID THEY HAVE PASTRAMI?
YES. EXTRA PICKLE.
AHHKKK!
SHIT!!

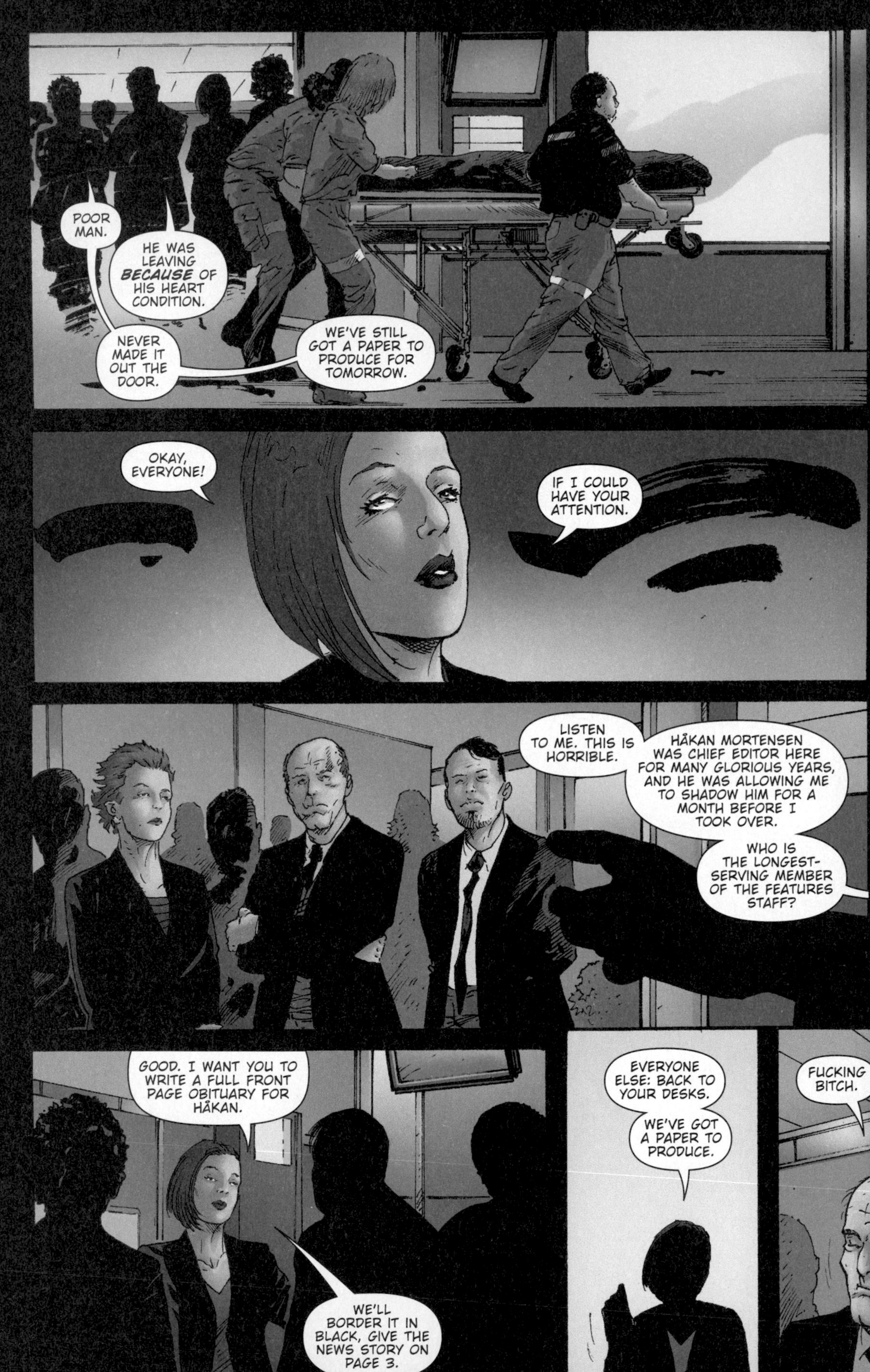

POOR MAN.
HE WAS LEAVING BECAUSE OF HIS HEART CONDITION.
NEVER MADE IT OUT THE DOOR.
WE'VE STILL GOT A PAPER TO PRODUCE FOR TOMORROW.
OKAY, EVERYONE!
IF I COULD HAVE YOUR ATTENTION.
LISTEN TO ME. THIS IS HORRIBLE.
HÅKAN MORTENSEN WAS CHIEF EDITOR HERE FOR MANY GLORIOUS YEARS, AND HE WAS ALLOWING ME TO SHADOW HIM FOR A MONTH BEFORE I TOOK OVER.
WHO IS THE LONGEST-SERVING MEMBER OF THE FEATURES STAFF?
GOOD. I WANT YOU TO WRITE A FULL FRONT PAGE OBITUARY FOR HÅKAN.
WE'LL BORDER IT IN BLACK, GIVE THE NEWS STORY ON PAGE 3.
EVERYONE ELSE: BACK TO YOUR DESKS.
WE'VE GOT A PAPER TO PRODUCE.
FUCKING BITCH.

"AREN'T YOU SUPPOSED TO WEAR ONE OF THEM?"
"YES."
DID YOU FORGET TO TAKE IT OFF?
I LEAVE THEM ON.
IN CASE THERE'S ANY LEFT.
LISBETH, I'VE BEEN COMING HERE FOR THREE WEEKS.
I KNOW YOU DON'T WANT TO TALK ABOUT IT.
THERE ARE BIG GAPS...
AUTHOR OF THE 1991 REPORT...
...DR. TELEBORIAN.
YOUR LEGAL GUARDIAN...
...ONE OF THE PEOPLE YOU'RE ACCUSED OF MURDERING.
AND NILS BJURMAN.

I UNDERSTAND THE HABIT OF SILENCE, LISBETH.
I KNOW WHERE IT COMES FROM.
IF WE TRY TO SPEAK AND FIND NO ONE LISTENS.
WE LEARN **NOT** TO SPEAK.
BUT YOU HAVE TO UNDERSTAND:
THE COURTS CANNOT TAKE ANYTHING INTO ACCOUNT...
...IF IT ISN'T PUT IN FRONT OF THEM.
IT BECOMES EASIER **NOT** TO SPEAK.
IT FEELS **SAFER** NOT TO SPEAK.
IT ISN'T SAFER.
IT'S CATASTROPHIC BECAUSE...
IN A COURT OF LAW **NOTHING** CAN BE INFERRED...
...YOU **HAVE** TO TELL.

THEN, IF WE MAKE THEM LISTEN...
THEY MAKE US TELL IT AS A *STORY.*
WITH GOOD GUYS AND BAD GUYS.
THE TRUTH IS ALWAYS MORE COMPLICATED.
I OFTEN THINK OF THIS QUOTE FROM JOYCE:
"ONE GREAT PART OF EVERY HUMAN EXISTENCE IS PASSED IN A STATE WHICH CANNOT BE RENDERED SENSIBLE BY THE USE OF WIDEAWAKE LANGUAGE, CUTANDDRY GRAMMAR AND GOAHEAD PLOT."
I NEED YOUR HELP.
YOU ***HAVE*** TO FIND A WAY TO TELL, LISBETH.
OR WE'LL LOSE THE CASE. YOUR STORY MAKES ***NO SENSE*** WITH THOSE PARTS MISSING.
THEY'LL ***HAVE*** TO FIND YOU INCOMPETENT. YOU'LL BE BACK IN THE CARE OF TELEBORIAN.

DR. JONASSON?
I'M DR. PETER TELEBORIAN.
I'M HERE TO VISIT MY PATIENT LISBETH SALANDER.
SALANDER IS MY PATIENT...HAS BEEN FOR A LONG TIME.
SO YOU SEE, YOU ARE LEGALLY OBLIGED TO GIVE ME ACCESS TO HER.
THIS IS AN EIGHT-YEAR-OLD LETTER FROM YOUR HOSPITAL BOARD.
GIVING ME LEGAL CUSTODY OF THE PATIENT--
YOU HAD CUSTODY OF HER THEN. YOU HAD CUSTODY OF HER THERE, TELEBORIAN.
HERE AND NOW SHE IS MY PATIENT.

WHEN SHE IS RELEASED INTO POLICE CUSTODY
I WILL ASSESS HER.
I HAVE A UNIQUE UNDER-STANDING OF THIS CASE.
I MUST SAY ON A PROFESSIONAL LEVEL...
YOUR BEHAVIOR IS NOT VERY COLLEGIATE.
NEITHER IS MUSCLING IN HERE WITH AN OUT-OF-DATE CUSTODY ORDER.
NEITHER IS WAITING THREE WEEKS TO SEND ME YOUR NOTES.
NEITHER WAS FINDING HALF OF THE NOTES MISSING, DOCTOR.
THOSE NOTES ARE TOP SECRET.
SHE IS A PARANOID SCHIZOPHRENIC.
IT'S ESSENTIAL THAT HER CONDITION IS NOT ALLOWED TO DETERIORATE--
--GET OUT!
YOU'RE NOT IN CHARGE OF MY PATIENT.
NOT UNTIL SHE'S DISCHARGED.

YOU KNOW DR. PETER TELEBORIAN?
...
TELEBORIAN CAME TO SEE ME.
...
HE WILL BE ASKED TO ASSESS YOU WHEN YOU'RE DISCHARGED.
SADLY, MISS SALANDER--
I DETECT A **MAJOR** SET-BACK IN YOUR CONDITION.
YOU'RE GOING **NOWHERE.**

OUR JUNE ISSUE IS A SPECIAL EDITION. SALANDER AND ZALA.
WE'RE DOING FIVE INTERRELATED ARTICLES. BLOWING THE LID OFF THE WHOLE STORY.
I'M COVERING THE ZALA DEFECTION AND SÄPO'S INVOLVEMENT.

ERIKSSON: YOU'RE WRITING UP THE MURDERS AT THE WAREHOUSE.
GOOD.
I'M ALSO WRITING UP THE TELEBORIAN AND BJURMAN INVOLVEMENT.
VERY UNFORTUNATE THAT WE DON'T HAVE THAT 1991 REPORT--
VERY UNFORTUNATE.

CORTEZ, CAN YOU TAKE THE--
NO.
NO?

SORRY, MIKEY, CAN YOU DO WITHOUT ME?
I'D LIKE TO STICK WITH THIS INVESTIGATION.
I'M RIGHT IN THE MIDDLE OF SOMETHING POTENTIALLY EXPLOSIVE.
WHAT ARE YOU IN THE MIDDLE OF?
TOILETS?

OKAY, WE CAN DO THE REST OURSELVES.
NOW, EVERYONE TO THE BAR FOR BEERS.
BEER? IT'S ONE THIRTY IN THE AFTERNOON!

REMEMBER: STAY OFF-GRID WITH THE REAL INVESTIGATION.
NO EMAILS.
NO IDLE CHAT IN THE OFFICE.
ASSUME EVERYTHING SAID IS BEING HEARD OR READ.
WE NEED TO SEEM NORMAL.
UNLESS YOU'RE IN THE STREET OR A PUBLIC PLACE.
MIL EN
KEEP TALKING AS YOU WOULD IF NOTHING WAS WRONG.
NO MENTION OF OUR REAL ACTIVITIES.
PAYG
NO, JUST GO TO THE BAR, MAKE IT SEEM LIKE A NORMAL, FRIENDLY STAFF DRINK.
TAKE THESE PHONES AND DISCARD ALL THE PACKAGING DISCREETLY.
MIKEY?
THESE ARE THE FLOOR PLANS AND HERE'S THE STAFF LIST.
HARD TO COME BY, ACTUALLY, BUT FULLY COMPRE-HENSIVE.
YOU'VE DONE A GREAT JOB.

BZZZ
3_ Black/White Publishing

MIKAEL BLOMKVIST!
MY DEAR FRIEND!
KURDO BAKSI! YOU OLD ROGUE!
HOW THE HELL ARE YOU?

IF YOU CAN MAKE TEA TASTE THIS INTENSE...
...IT'S A SHAME KURDS DON'T MAKE ALCOHOL.
SOME KURDS DO. ALL HOME-MADE.

TRUST ME, MIKEY,
IT IS LIKE DRINKING OMO.

SO, I KNOW YOU'RE NOT HERE TO TALK DHEW AND MASTOW.
WHAT CAN I DO FOR YOU?

I'M TRYING TO FIND SOMEONE: "IDRIS GHIDI."
WORKS AT SAHLGRENSKA HOSPITAL--
OH NO!

NO, MIKEY.
WHATEVER IT IS, ***NO.***
I HAVEN'T TOLD YOU WHY I WANT--

WHATEVER YOU WANT. THAT FAMILY HAS BEEN THROUGH ENOUGH.
HE WAS AN ENGINEER WITH A PH.D, NOW HE'S WORKING AS A HOSPITAL PORTER.
THE MAN CAN BARELY WALK.
MAYBE I WANT TO GIVE HIM A LOT OF MONEY.

IT'S NEVER GOOD, MIKEY...
NOT WHEN YOU COME TO ME LIKE THIS.

YOU ***CANNOT*** ASK HIM TO DO ***ANYTHING*** ILLEGAL.

IT IS NOT ILLEGAL.
IT'S LEAVING A *PHONE* IN A *CUPBOARD*.
SK 1000 A WEEK TO RECHARGE IT.

BACK IN IRAQ THE GHIDI FAMILY WAS SUSPECTED OF BEING KURDISH MILITANTS.
SADDAM'S POLICE HELD IDRIS. THEY TORTURED HIM FOR ELEVEN MONTHS.
THEY ONLY LET HIM OUT BECAUSE THEY THOUGHT HE WOULD DIE. AND BEFORE THEY DID--
--THEY SMASHED HIS HIP WITH A SLEDGE HAMMER.

IF YOU GET HIM INTO TROUBLE HE WILL BE SENT *BACK* TO IRAQ.

I'LL GIVE HIM *YOUR* NUMBER. HE CAN CALL OR NOT CALL.
AND IF ANYTHING HAPPENS TO HIM, I'LL BREAK *YOUR* LEGS.
Folet
Fredriksson
Ghidi
Gronkjaer
Gud
Gunnar F.
YOU'RE WARY. I GET IT, BAKSI.

--AND RECHARGE IT ONCE A WEEK?
I'LL TELL YOU WHEN IT'S OVER.
AND THEN YOU CAN KEEP THE HANDSET.

WET
LOOR

TWENTY MINUTES LATE, HOLM.
I HAVE IMPORTANT WORK TO DO.
SIT DOWN.

I'VE GOT WORK TO DO.
WHAT DO YOU WANT?

OKAY, IF THAT'S WHAT YOU WANT: YOUR WORK ISN'T GOOD ENOUGH. YOU IGNORE MY EDITS.
YOUR NEWS STORIES ARE FULL OF OPINION...
AND YOU'RE LATE FOR *EVERY-THING*.

HOW DARE YOU SPEAK TO ME LIKE THAT!
HOW DARE YOU BE TWENTY MINUTES LATE!
MY WORK HAS NEVER BEEN CALLED INTO QUESTION.

IN HERE.
"SALANDER: SUSPECT IN DOUBLE SLAYING. SOLD STEROIDS IN BOXING GYM"?
I CUT THAT STORY!

THAT'S A JOURNALIST ASKING THE RIGHT QUESTION.
I WOULDN'T BE ANGRY, HOLM IF I DIDN'T THINK YOU WERE CAPABLE OF MORE!
SHAPE UP OR GET OUT, HOLM.
WE DON'T HAVE ROOM FOR PASSENGERS HERE.
I'LL OUTLAST YOU, BERGER.
THANKS FOR COMING IN, FRISK.
I WANT TO EMPLOY YOU IN A ONE-OFF CONTRACT.
YOU KNOW I'M ALWAYS LOOKING FOR WORK, ERIKA.
FEEDING PREJUDICIAL SNIPPETS TO MY REPORTERS.
WHO ARE THEY COMING FROM?
WHO'S BEHIND THE ANTI-SALANDER STORIES?
D'YOU THINK IT'S SÄPO?
I DON'T WANT TO *GUESS*.
I WANT TO *KNOW*.

VITAVARA INC.
LUXURY IN EVERY DETAIL

FABRICATED IN SWEATSHOP CONDITIONS USING SLAVE LABOR.
SOLD ON THROUGH A HOLDING COMPANY *TRIPLING* THE MARKUP...
...AND THE SUBSEQUENT PRICE.
SOLID SIX *HUNDRED* PERCENT PROFIT.
WOW, YEAH?
WHY IS THAT A "WOW"?
IT'S WRONG, BUT HOW IS IT A STORY?

THE ZALACHENKO AFFAIR.
IT'S STILL A MATTER OF THE HIGHEST NATIONAL SECURITY.
IF THIS COMES OUT.
--THAT HE DEFECTED HERE AT THE HEIGHT OF THE COLD WAR--
THEY'LL KNOW WHAT HE TOLD US.
OUR AGENTS IN RUSSIA WILL BE IN DANGER.
THEY'D KILL THEM?
ALMOST CERTAINLY.
YOU HAVE NO IDEA HOW POWERFUL THESE PEOPLE ARE...
...OR WHAT THEY WOULD DO TO PROTECT THEMSELVES.
WE CAN'T TRUST MANY PEOPLE WITH THIS.
BUT WE'VE BEEN WATCHING YOU FOR QUITE SOME TIME. WE KNOW YOU'RE A TRUSTWORTHY MAN.

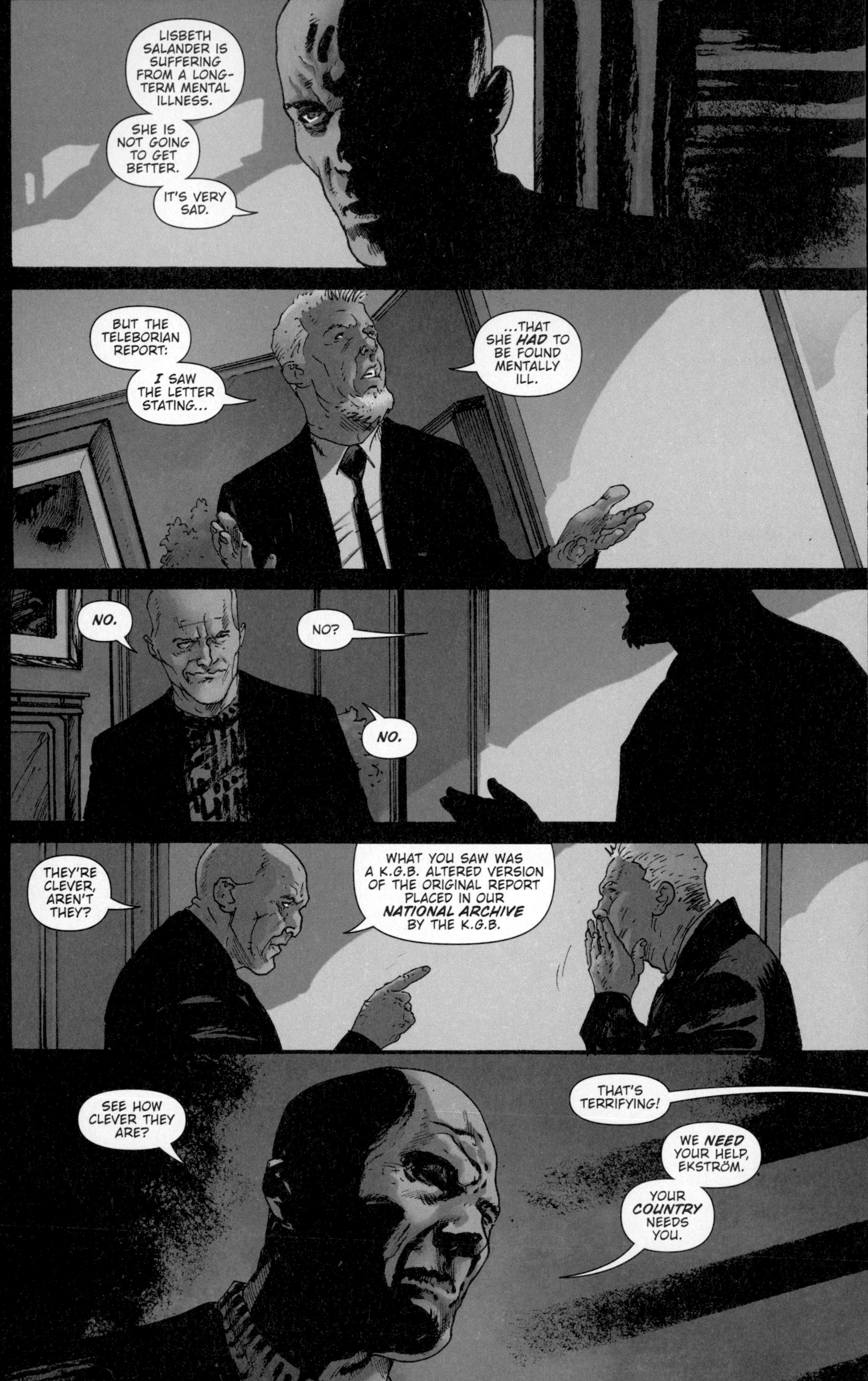
LISBETH SALANDER IS SUFFERING FROM A LONG-TERM MENTAL ILLNESS.
SHE IS NOT GOING TO GET BETTER.
IT'S VERY SAD.
BUT THE TELEBORIAN REPORT:
I SAW THE LETTER STATING...
...THAT SHE HAD TO BE FOUND MENTALLY ILL.
NO.
NO?
NO.
THEY'RE CLEVER, AREN'T THEY?
WHAT YOU SAW WAS A K.G.B. ALTERED VERSION OF THE ORIGINAL REPORT PLACED IN OUR NATIONAL ARCHIVE BY THE K.G.B.
SEE HOW CLEVER THEY ARE?
THAT'S TERRIFYING!
WE NEED YOUR HELP, EKSTRÖM.
YOUR COUNTRY NEEDS YOU.

HAVING EXPANDED TO INCLUDE SEVERAL DIFFERENT LINES OF INQUIRY.
SEVERAL MURDER INVESTIGATIONS... THIS MAY OR MAY NOT BE CONNECTED.
I HAVE COME TO THE CONCLUSION THAT THE ONLY WAY TO PROCEED IS A REORGANIZATION OF THE ENTIRE INVESTIGATION.
AS OF NOW, HANS FASTE WILL BE INVESTIGATING SALANDER, BJÖRCK AND SÄPO TRAILS.
YOU WILL BE PURSUING THE NIEDERMANN INQUIRY. IT MUST BE SUSPECTED THAT HE HAS LEFT SWEDEN.
WHERE HAS HE GONE? GERMANY? FINLAND?
WE NEED TO FIND VIKTOR GÖRANSSON'S SAAB--
YOU DON'T UNDERSTAND, PROSECUTOR EKSTRÖM:
THERE HAS BEEN A CONSPIRACY AGAINST LISBETH SALANDER.
SINCE AT LEAST 1991--

AH, THE '91 TELEBORIAN REPORT.
INSPECTOR BUBLANSKI, I'M AFRAID IT'S YOU WHO DOES NOT UNDERSTAND.
I HAVE IT ON THE HIGHEST POSSIBLE AUTHORITY THAT REPORT WAS FALSIFIED.
FALSIFIED?
YES, FALSIFIED.
AND THE ONLY MAN WHO COULD HAVE CONTRADICTED THAT: BJÖRCK.
JUST HAPPENS TO HAVE DIED UNDER MYSTERIOUS CIRCUMSTANCES?
FALSIFIED?
WE CAN'T LET THIS HAPPEN TO HER AGAIN.
EKSTRÖM HAS MY COPY OF THE '91 REPORT!
I CAN'T EVEN PROVE IT EXISTED.
I'VE STILL GOT ONE. I COPIED MINE.

DRAGAN ARMANSKY.
THANK YOU FOR COMING.
WHY THE SECRECY?
BECAUSE I KNOW YOU'RE A FRIEND OF LISBETH SALANDER'S.
COMING TO YOU GOES AGAINST EVERYTHING I BELIEVE IN, DRAGAN. I BELIEVE IN THE SYSTEM, IN ORDER.
HOWEVER FLAWED. BUT EVENTS ARE OVERTAKING US. BUT POWERFUL FORCES ARE ALIGNING AGAINST LISBETH SALANDER.
IF I DIDN'T COME TO YOU WARN YOU...
...I FEEL AS IF I MIGHT NEVER SLEEP AGAIN.

MY BOSS TOOK THE 1991 PSYCHIATRIC REPORT. THE ONLY PROOF THAT SHE WAS SET UP.
THE DAY BJÖRCK DIED. EVERY EXISTING COPY OF THE REPORT WAS STOLEN.
PEOPLE WERE MUGGED OR BURGLED. THEY'RE ALL GONE.
BUT NOW HANS FASTE, THE ONE OFFICER WHO HATES SALANDER...
...HAS BEEN PUT IN CHARGE OF HER CASE. IT HAS TO BE AN ORCHESTRATED CAMPAIGN.
AND IT COULD ONLY BE RUN BY SOMEONE INCREDIBLY HIGH UP.
I DIDN'T KNOW THEY HAD THAT SORT OF PULL.
"BLOMKVIST CALLS THEM THE 'ZALA CLUB.' THEY'RE A SMALL GROUP OF DORMANT COLD WARMONGERS.
"HIDING IN A CORNER OF SÄPO."
I'M AFRAID FOR HER, DRAGAN, I'M AFRAID FOR ALL OF US.
THEY'RE OFF THE GRID AND THEY'RE DESPERATE.
YOU'RE RIGHT TO BE AFRAID, BUBLANSKI. WE'RE ALL IN DANGER.

SHE'S TRAPPED.
SHE'S THE ONLY ONE WHO CAN GATHER THE EVIDENCE SHE NEEDS TO DEFEND HERSELF.
THAT'S WHY SHE'S BEING HELD INCOMMUNICADO.
WHY NOT GIVE IT TO HER LAWYER?
LISBETH HASN'T TOLD HER LAWYER EVERYTHING.
I THINK SHE HAS THE RIGHT TO INVESTIGATE THE CASE HERSELF.
IT'S ENTIRELY UP TO YOU.

NORMALLY I WOULDN'T COME STRAIGHT TO YOU.
BUT EVERY OTHER CHANNEL IS BLOCKED, AS YOU CAN SEE.
ARE ANY OF THESE ALLEGATIONS DOCUMENTED?

TORSTEN EDKLINTH
DIRECTOR OF
CONSTITUTIONAL PROTECTION
SECURITY SERVICES
COME IN!
MONICA, YOU READ THE FILE?
I DID, SIR.
IF THERE IS ANYTHING IN IT...
WE HAVE A CONSTITUTIONAL CRISIS ON OUR HANDS.
WE NEED PROOF. I WANT YOU TO INVESTIGATE.
THIS NEEDS TO BE UNDER THE RADAR...LEAVE NO TRACE OF WHAT YOU'RE DOING.
LOOK AT THE PHONE TAPING AT THE MILLENNIUM OFFICES...WHO IS FOLLOWING MIKAEL BLOMKVIST.
EVERT GULLBERG: WHO WAS *HE*?
AND OFFICER FIGUEROA?
SIR?
THE '91 PSYCHIATRIC REPORT, FIND OUT WHAT YOU CAN ABOUT THE PEOPLE INVOLVED.
SIR.

HI, PERSONNEL?
YEAH, WE NEED A PSYCH REPORT DONE ON SOMEONE.
DR. PETER TELEBORIAN OF ST. STEPHAN'S.
IS HE CLEARED TO HANDLE CLASSIFIED INFORMATION?
HE IS?
THANK YOU.
SI Volvo 1991 grey
Mårtensson, Göran SIS
Personal Protection
SECONDED: COUNTER-ESPIONAGE
AVAILABLE FOR RE-SECONDMENT TO US IN CONSTITUTIONAL PROTECTION?
HE'S NOT WITH YOU IN COUNTER-ESPIONAGE?
MY MISTAKE. I DO APOLOGIZE.
WE'VE GOT A CRISIS, SIR.

...FALLING PROFITS CAUSING SHAREHOLDERS' DIVIDENDS TO DROP.
WE HAVE TO CUT COSTS TO RETAIN PROFITABILITY... WE'LL BE CUTTING STAFF--
--NO!
NO, MAGNUS. WE'RE *NOT* MAKING STAFF CUTS.
IT HAS BEEN DONE TIME AND TIME AGAIN. WE'RE LOSING CONTENT...
...WRITING QUALITY--ALL TO MEET THE DIVIDEND.
HOW DO YOU SUGGEST WE--
CUT BOARD BONUSES!
...*MINIMIZE* DIVIDENDS. WE PRODUCE A SMALLER PAPER WITH FEWER ADVERTS.
WE CONCENTRATE ON PRODUCING A GREAT PAPER THAT PEOPLE *NEED* TO READ.
YOU MEAN REPRODUCE MILLENNIUM?
NO, THAT'S NOT WHAT I MEAN.
RADICAL FOR RADICAL'S SAKE. SHAREHOLDERS WOULD SELL, CAUSE A SHARE PRICE CRASH.
A SHARE PRICE CRASH IS BETTER THAN A SLOW DEATH BY STRANGULATION!

NOT HAPPY?
THEY CAN'T HEAR ME. AS SOON AS I SAID "NO BONUS"...
...THEY ALL WENT SELECTIVELY DEAF.
and rape you, fucking bitch.
I CAN TELL THAT IT HAS BEEN SENT FROM *INSIDE* THE PAPER.
IT'S ODD, THOUGH... THE ADDRESS IS UNTRACEABLE.
and rape you, fucking bitch.
THE ADDRESS HAS BEEN SET UP ONLY FOR THIS. THIS IS THE ONLY EMAIL THAT HAS EVER BEEN SENT FROM HERE...
AND IT WAS SET UP THIS MORNING.

MIKAEL: TOILETS.
HOW'S IT GOING?
THERE'S A BIG PROBLEM.

VITAVARA INC.
IT'S OWNED BY A MEMBER OF THE BOARD ON SMP.

OH SHIT.
ONE OF ERIKA BERGER'S BOSSES?
MAGNUS BORGSJÖ. DO YOU THINK IT WILL BE AN ISSUE?

BORGSJÖ ISN'T ONE OF HER BOSSES.
BORGSJÖ IS THE MAN WHO HEADHUNTED HER.

ARE WE BUMPING THE STORY?
NO. NO, WE CAN'T.
LEAVE IT TO ME, I'LL TALK TO HER.

"DR. TELEBORIAN CAME TO SEE YOU. DO YOU KNOW HIM?"
"HE'S A BASTARD."
"HE'S CERTAINLY CONVINCED OF HIS OWN SIGNIFICANCE."
EMERGENCY
HE SAID HE WAS DOING AN ASSESSMENT OF YOU?
HE'S FILLING OUT THE PAPER-WORK TO SAY I'M MENTALLY ILL.
THAT'S NOT AN ASSESSMENT. THAT'S A TRAP.
YOU'VE GOT A SERIOUS HEALTH PROBLEM, LISBETH. BUT YOU'RE GETTING BETTER FAR TOO QUICKLY.
THE MINUTE I SIGN YOUR RELEASE FORM, YOU'LL BE TRANSFERRED TO PRISON.
AND TELEBORIAN WILL START THAT PROCESS.
I'M AFRAID YOU HAVE A SLIGHT TEMPERATURE. VERY CONCERNING.
WE'LL HAVE TO DEFER YOUR RELEASE...
...KEEP YOU HERE FOR OBSERVATION... A FEW WEEKS AT LEAST.

CIDLA
My email being hacked.
You:
pippi-p9i2p7p7i@yehoo.com
bx
SAVE

IDIOT...
THERE'S NO INTERNET HERE ANYWAY...
WORK
KALLE

://www.trhare.se/ X

CLICK

Welcome to the Hackers Republic
citizen Wasp...

...

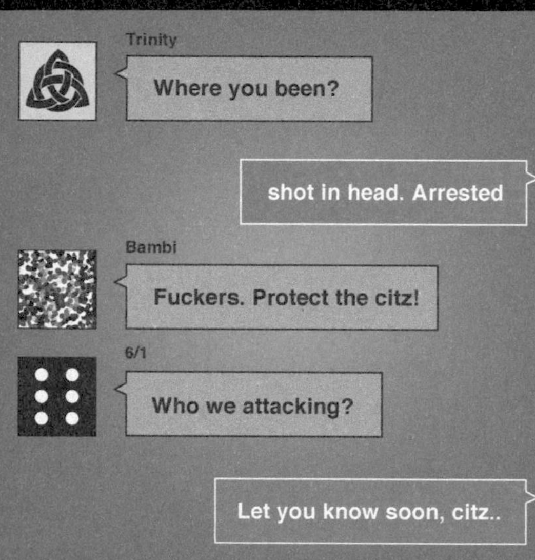

Trinity
Where you been?
shot in head. Arrested
Bambi
Fuckers. Protect the citz!
6/1
Who we attacking?
Let you know soon, citz..

Their armies are massing on the border.

Disengagement is for defenseless children. You need to fight this one.

Dr.T is their central point of attack. You need to tell your story. If you can't speak it write it. Otherwise Dr.T will win.

FIGHT

BLOMKVIST
HOME ADDRESS ↑
JOURNALIST
TWO MEN IN A CAB
WAITING 18 MINS
NOT LUNCH TIME
LARS FAULSSON
Lock and Key Services
UNKNOWN OPERATIVE

Key Services

FOUND THE REG?
A POLICE OFFICER?
NO, IT'S WEIRD THOUGH: SHE SEEMS TO BE WATCHING *THEM*, NOT *ME*.

Riddargatan
Kaptensgatan
Riddargatan
Hotel Diplomat
Strandvagen
Strandvagen
Strandvagen
Nybroviken
Stallgatan
Blasieholmen
MILTON SECURITY
YES, SHE WAS GREAT. WE'D LIKE TO HIRE HER AGAIN.
YES, FOR PERSONAL PROTECTION. YOU KNOW, IT'S *TERRIBLE* BUT I CANNOT RECALL HER NAME!
WOMAN, LATE TWENTIES, BLACK BOB? "SUZANNE LINDER"?
THANKS *SO* MUCH! WE'LL FINALIZE THE DATES AND GET BACK IN TOUCH.

SIR?
FIGUEROA.
FIND ANYTHING?
FALUN: CROOK, BURGLAR, STRONG OF CONVICTIONS.
MÅRTENSSON: SECONDED TO SECURITY SERVICE JOB THAT DOESN'T EXIST.
THIS IS REALLY SERIOUS. I'M STARTING TO THINK IT MIGHT ALL BE TRUE.
MIGHT BE...
BLOMKVIST RAN YOUR REGISTRATION, INCIDENTALLY.
KEEP USING YOUR CAR BUT REMEMBER: HE KNOWS WHO AND WHAT YOU ARE.
THE PLACE WAS CRAWLING WITH OPERATIVES.
HE MUST ALREADY KNOW WHO THE OTHER ONES ARE.
...PRETTY SMART...

GUSTAV'S
PUB & KÖK
CLICK
SUKA

CITY CORNER
SNACK BAR & TAKE AWAY ORDERS TAKEN
YOU HAVE NO AUTHORITY.
THERE IS NO REASON ON EARTH WHY I SHOULD TALK TO YOU OR TRUST YOU.
I KNOW.
CORRECT.
YOUR I.D. SAYS YOU ARE A MEMBER OF *S.I.S.*.
TO BE HONEST, YOU'RE THE LAST PEOPLE I TRUST RIGHT NOW.
I'M NOT EVEN SURE I HAVE JURISDICTION TO ASK YOU ABOUT IT.
SOMETHING HAS HAPPENED IN OUR DIVISION.
THE GENERATION INVOLVED HAS MORE OR LESS MOVED ON.
MY GENERATION DOESN'T KNOW ABOUT IT.
WE'RE MORE OR LESS MAPPING VAPOR TRAILS IN CLOUDS.
I'M TRYING TO WORK OUT WHAT THOSE TRAILS COME FROM.
AND YOU WANT ME TO HELP YOU?
I'D LIKE YOU TO TELL ME ABOUT THE ZALACHENKO CASE.
EVERYTHING AND ANYTHING.

MIKEY, I MISS YOU...
OH, RICKY.
WEEKS.
FEELS LIKE A YEAR!

WORST JOB I'VE EVER HAD.
THE STAFF HATES ME. I HATE MOST OF THEM BACK. I'M GETTING ANONYMOUS THREATS--
I THINK I NEED A GIRLFRIEND, RICKY.
YOU'RE MAKING ME MORE MISERABLE.
THEN WHY ARE YOU GRINNING?

I JUST SAW SOMETHING THAT MADE ME LAUGH.
WHAT?
YOUR FACE.

IT'S TOO MUCH FOR ONE JOB. NO WONDER THE PREVIOUS EDITOR HAD A HEART ATTACK.

COME AND WORK WITH ME, MIKEY. I CAN OFFER YOU A SUB ED POSITION.
TWICE WHAT YOU GET AT MILLENNIUM?
NO, RICKY. MY DAYS OF WORKING WITH PEOPLE I HATE ARE OVER.
I JUST DON'T HAVE THE TEMPERAMENT.

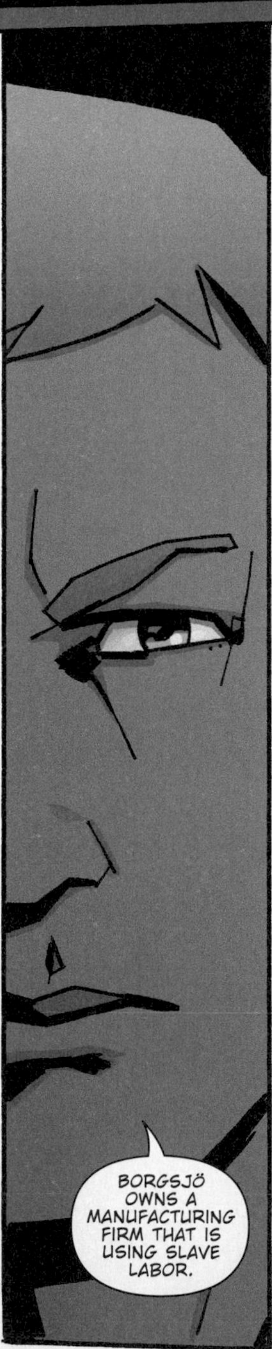
BORGSJÖ OWNS A MANUFACTURING FIRM THAT IS USING SLAVE LABOR.

MY BOSS BORGSJÖ? BORGSJÖ, THE MAN WHO GAVE ME THIS JOB?
YES.
THE ***MINUTE*** I LEAVE?!?
--NO, RICKY. THAT'S NOT WHAT HAPPENED.
YOU INVESTIGATE THE PEOPLE I'M--
CORTEZ WAS INVESTIGATING ***VITAVARA***. WE HAD ***NO IDEA*** BORGSJÖ WAS INVOLVED.

IF YOU PRINT THIS, SMP'S SHARE PRICE WILL FALL THROUGH THE FLOOR.
I KNOW. THAT'S WHY I'M TELLING YOU.
THAT WOULD MEAN LAYOFFS.
I MIGHT **HATE** THEM BUT I DON'T WANT TO **SACK** THEM.
ANDERS HOLMS STILL THERE?
HE'S ONE OF THE BIGGEST PAINS IN MY ARSE.
GOOD JOURNALIST, CAR CRASH PERSONALITY.
HE WAS ACCUSED OF SEXUAL HARASSMENT BACK IN THE DAY.
WAS HE?
NOTHING PROVED.
BUT AN ACCUSATION WAS SO RARE BACK THEN...
I NEED TO GET BORGSJÖ TO STAND DOWN FROM THE BOARD.
CAN YOU GIVE ME A MONTH?
I WAS GOING TO OFFER YOU TWO.

HOW ARE YOU FEELING, LISBETH?
OKAY.
SAME.
SHE SHOULD BE RELEASED INTO *MY* CUSTODY!
WELL, HER TEMPERATURE IS UP AND DOWN.
AND ON THAT BASIS I'M UNDER AN OBLIGATION--
--TO KEEP HER IN FOR OBSERVATION.
YOU CAN'T KEEP HER FROM CUSTODY FOR-EVER! SHE'S *MY* PRISONER, NOT *YOURS*.

I'M NOT SURE YOU UNDERSTAND WHAT HOSPITALS ARE FOR, OFFICER FASTE.
I'M CALLING PROSECUTOR EDKLINTH!
I THINK YOU SHOULD LEAVE NOW.
I am Lisbeth Salander. I was bo
on the 30th April 1978. My mother
was seventeen when she had me.
Her name was Agneta Sofia
Salander. My father was Alexander
Zalachenko. He was a psychopathic
wife beater, a spy and a murder.
He was an agent for the K.G.B
and defected to the West
WILL NOT TOLERATE PRISONERS BEING HELD WITHOUT--
SECURITY, PLEASE?!
MY PATIENT HAS HAD ONE ATTEMPT ON HER LIFE IN THIS WARD ALREADY.
HER HEALTH IS PRECARIOUS AND YOU ARE NOT HELPING.
You dead yet?
a bit.
You dead yet?
a bit.

Need help.
Need money.
30k?
Ok. What's the job?
Get Trinity to Stockholm
Someone's phone being bugged then?
Millennium mag and Mikuel Blomkvist
both bugged.
find but don't destroy

SNORING!
LIKE A TRACTOR!
LET'S NOT LEAVE IT SO LONG NEXT TIME.
BYE, MIKEY.
BITCH

ALARMING!
SUPERFICIALLY.
WE DON'T HAVE THE POWERS TO INVESTIGATE ALL OF THESE DIFFERENT DEPARTMENTS IN DEPTH.
IN FACT, NO ONE DOES.
QUITE RIGHT, MONICA: SUPERFICIALLY...
VERY, VERY, VERY ALARMING.
9 PM? WE'LL BE THERE.

THE PRIME MINISTER'S READY A LITTLE BIT EARLY.
COME ON IN.
WE CAN FIND NO RECORDS OF EVERT GULLBERG EXISTING BEYOND THE MOST SUPERFICIAL LEVEL.
BUT THE REAL PROBLEM IS THE DIFFERENT DEPARTMENTS WHO ARE INVOLVED. WE DO NOT HAVE THE AUTHORITY TO INVESTIGATE S.I.S.
MUCH LESS A SUSPECTED SHADOW CELL.
BUT IF WE ARE RIGHT, THEN THEY ARE BREAKING THE CONSTITUTION.
AND THEY ARE DOING IT SPECIFICALLY TO STAGE-MANAGE THE PROSECUTION OF LISBETH SALANDER.
WE WILL BE IN BREACH OF THE CONSTITUTION IF WE STOP THIS CASE FROM GOING BEFORE A CRIMINAL COURT.
THE CASE MUST BE PROSECUTED.
MISS FIGUEROLA, I WONDER--
NO.
THIS IS EXTRAORDINARY AUTHORIZATION.
GRANTING TIME-LIMITED POWERS TO INVESTIGATE.
I MAY NOT BE ABLE TO DECIDE WHETHER OR NOT SHE IS JUDICIALLY SANE.
BUT I DO HAVE THE POWER TO ENSURE...
...YOU GET ACCESS TO ALL OF THE AVAILABLE INFORMATION.

PRIME MINISTER FÄLLDIN. I DIDN'T KNOW IF YOU WOULD REMEMBER ME.
WELL, JERKER HOLMBERG, YOU LOOK SO MUCH LIKE GUSTAV.
I REMEMBER YOUR FATHER A LITTLE BETTER, OF COURSE.
SO, YOU'RE A POLICE OFFICER, DOWN IN STOCKHOLM NOW?
YES, SIR.
AND HOW DO YOU LIKE THAT?
THAT'S ACTUALLY WHY I'M HERE.
I WORK UNDER INSPECTOR BUBLANSKI OF THE VIOLENT CRIMES DIVISION.
HE DOESN'T KNOW I'M HERE. I'D BE IN A LOT OF TROUBLE IF ANYONE KNEW.
BUT I'M AFRAID THAT IF I DON'T DO SOMETHING, A TERRIBLE INJUSTICE WILL BE REPEATED.
I'M HONORED THAT YOU TRUST ME. REST ASSURED: WHATEVER YOU SAY HERE...
...WILL BE TREATED IN STRICTEST CONFIDENCE AND IF I CAN HELP, I WILL.

DRIVING ON THE RIGHT, ON THE RIGHT, ON THE RIGHT...
YOU CAN HACK FUCKING NATO.
BUT THIS YOU FIND DIFFICULT?
SMOKE'S JUST COMING STRAIGHT BACK IN.
STINKS IN HERE NOW.
WELL LET'S STOP THEN. LET ME HAVE ME LUXURY SMOKES.
WITHOUT ALL THESE LITTLE BITS BLOODY FLOATING BACK IN AT ME.
WE CAN'T STOP, MATE.
ONE OF THE REPUBLIC'S CITIZENS NEEDS US.
STOP BLOODY MOANING THEN.
PLAGUE? YEAH.
THE CAVALRY'S ARRIVED.
YEAH, WE BOTH NEED SHOWERS AND A POO.

DO YOU NEED HELP TO GET BACK INTO BED?
NO.
OKAY.
Surveillance by Mårtensson
Police on sp ops
Send me all files
and CC to Kalle at his private address.
freaky stuff on Dr. T's hard drive.
...Kids and stuff.
No Surprise.
Do something with it.

London friends are working hard. Already in Prosecutor Ekström's email. They will forward copies of it all to you.
WHAT?

SONJA MODIG!
I HAD GIVEN UP ON YOU CONTACTING ME.
I KNOW WHO EVERT GULLBERG IS.
THIS COULD BE VERY DANGEROUS... YOU DON'T KNOW WHO THESE PEOPLE ARE, BLOMKVIST.
I WILL GO TO JAIL BEFORE I REVEAL MY SOURCES.
IT'S A COLLEAGUE OF MINE.
I'D RATHER NOT SAY HIS NAME.
I NEED TO KNOW MY SOURCES TO PROTECT THEM.
I ALSO NEED TO KNOW IT ISN'T SOMEONE PLANTING EVIDENCE, SONJA.
HOP!

JERKER HOLMBERG.
HIS FATHER IS OLD FRIENDS WITH THORBJÖRN FÄLLDIN,
PRIME MINISTER AT THE TIME OF THE ZALACHENKO DEFECTION.
HOLMBERG WENT TO SEE HIM.
FÄLLDIN DIDN'T WANT TO TALK.
BUT AGE MAKES MEN RECKLESS SOMETIMES...
FÄLLDIN TOLD HOLMBERG THAT SÄPO HANDLED IT ALL.
THEY BUILT A WALL AROUND IT, TO SEPARATE IT FROM THE EXECUTIVE. IF THE RUSSIANS FOUND OUT, THERE COULD BE A WAR...
BUT FÄLLDIN WAS CAUTIOUS, HE INSISTED ON ONE POINT OF CONTACT.
A **GO-BETWEEN** TO KEEP HIM INFORMED WHILE KEEPING THE GOVERNMENT INSULATED.
JANERYD. HOLMBERG MET HIM.
JANERYD DEALT DIRECTLY WITH THE HEAD OF THE SPECIAL ZALA UNIT: EVERT GULLBERG.

EVERT GULLBERG.
YOU COULDN'T IDENTIFY HIM?
THAT'S RIGHT, PRIME MINISTER.
NEITHER COULD WE. BUT YOU WERE RIGHT.
HIS BIOGRAPHY IS VERY THIN... TOO THIN.
AS IF IT HAS BEEN PROFESSIONALLY THINNED. IT TAKES A LOT OF MOTIVATION TO DO THAT.
AND ACCESS TO VERY SENSITIVE AREAS OF GOVERNMENT. HE HAD FRIENDS IN HIGH PLACES...
SO WE LOOKED AT THE HIGHEST PLACE.
THE VISITOR'S LOG BOOK FOR THE PRIME MINISTER'S RESIDENCE 1990-1991.

log out 00.58
MULTIPLE ENTRIES BEFORE THE DEFECTION.
IMMEDIATELY AFTERWARDS: ***NOTHING***.
EVER AGAIN.
IT'S KIND OF EXTRAORDINARY.
THE DEVOTION HE SHOWED...
...ONE DAY EVERT GULLBERG KNEW ***EVERYONE***.
ZALACHENKO DECIDES TO DEFECT.
...CONTACTS SÄPO AND--
--NO ONE EVER HEARS FROM GULLBERG AGAIN.
UNTIL HE SHOOTS ZALA DEAD AND TURNS THE GUN ON HIMSELF.

WHAT IS IT?
CAN'T YOU SEE?
ALL I SEE IS DATES, MONICA.
DATES. TIMES.
FROM SÄPO'S CORRESPONDENCE RECEIPT BOOK!
DON'T ASK ME HOW I GOT THEM!
BUT, WHAT ARE THESE LOGS OF?
THE THREATENING LETTERS EVERT GULLBERG WROTE.
THE ONES THEY ANNOUNCED RIGHT AFTER HE SHOT ZALACHENKO.
THEY RECEIVED THEM TWO DAYS AFTER THE SHOOTING.
THEY ANNOUNCED THEM THE DAY BEFORE THEY ACTUALLY GOT THEM.
IF BLOMKVIST PUBLISHES THIS STORY BEFORE WE'VE FINISHED, HE COULD BLOW THE WHOLE INVESTIGATION.

BITCH
DRAGAN ARMANSKY?
HI, DRAGAN, SORRY TO CALL, BUT I MIGHT NEED A LITTLE PROTECTION.
I AM SUZANNE LINDER. DRAGAN SENT ME.
I'VE CONDUCTED A PERIMETER SEARCH AND FOUND THE POINT OF ENTRY.
I'LL STAY HERE AS LONG AS YOU NEED ME.

DID YOU CHECK YOUR SAFE?
IS ANYTHING MISSING?
YES.
A DVD OF A PERSONAL NATURE.
STARRING ME, MY HUSBAND, AND ANOTHER MAN.
AND A FILE ABOUT THE COMMERCIAL ACTIVITIES OF ONE OF OUR BOARD MEMBERS.
BITCH
BORGSJÖ IN TODAY, FREDRIKSSON?
NOT TODAY, BOSS.
I GOT ANOTHER "WHORE" EMAIL.
ERIKA, WE NEED TO DO SOMETHING.
THERE MUST BE A WAY OF FINDING OUT WHO'S SENDING THEM.
your tape. You a
me. Did you like
mess I made in yo
house? You should
raped by
Poison Pen is in your office. I have friends who can find them. Give us access to your SMPs

WHERE CAN I DROP YOU?
ANY RESTAURANT.
I'M STARVING.
ME TOO.
ERIKA BERGER IS YOUR LOVER?
SOMETIMES.
YOUR MARRIAGE BROKE UP OVER HER.
MY MARRIAGE WOULDN'T HAVE WORKED ANYWAY.
STILL NO SIGN OF RONALD NIEDERMANN?
NOT A TRACE.
NOT A RIPPLE, NOT A HAIR.

Dr. Nicolas Grünmer
To: Fwd.: Dr. Teleborian:
Re: the recent report of the Psychiatric
Elias Honsbel
Re: Thursday meeting has been moved to
Dr. Nicolas Grünmer
To: Dr. Teleborian:
Re: the recent report of the Psychiatric
Jonas Sandeberg: URGENT
3pm Saturday Circle Café.
Dr. Nicolas Grünmer
Dr. Teleborian:
Re: the recent report of the Psychiatric
14:18
LISBETH?
DR. PLEASE. URGENT.
WHAT IS IT?
LEND ME YOUR MOBILE.
I'M NOT ALLOWED TO DO THAT, LIS--
NO TIME! PLEASE?!
ERIKA BERGER?
I NEED YOU TO GET A MESSAGE URGENTLY TO MIKAEL--
NO.
I TRIED TO--
TAKE THE *FUCKING MESSAGE!*
MIKEY?
LISBETH PHONED TO SAY:
TELEBORIAN IS MEETING JONAS SANDEBERG IN FIFTEEN MINUTES--

BAR
YOU TAKE THE DOCTOR.

BUBLANSKI? I'VE JUST FOLLOWED TELEBORIAN TO YOUR OFFICE.
HE'S MEETING SOMEONE IN THERE...HAVE YOU GOT *ANYONE* IN THERE?
YES, WHO'D BE WORKING ON A SATURDAY?

CLICK!
CLICK!
CLICK!
CLICK!
CLICK!

SANDEBERG AND MÅRTENSSON ARE LISTED AS POLICE PERSONNEL.
BOTH ARE LISTED AS WORKING IN DIFFERENT OVERSEAS OFFICES.
NEITHER HAS EVER BEEN SEEN THERE. THE APARTMENT BLOCK HAS A FLAT OWNED BY A COMPANY.
"HANS WILHELM FRANCKE"--A KNOWN COVER COMPANY FOR S.I.S.
THIS IS WHAT TELEBORIAN WAS GIVING TO EKSTRÖM LAST NIGHT.
MODIG MADE A COPY.
WHAT IS IT?
HIS PSYCHIATRIC REPORT ON SALANDER.
NOTHING WRONG WITH THAT.
IT SEEMS TO BE IN ORDER.
YOU WOULD EXPECT HIM TO SHARE IT WITH THE PROSECUTION.
YEAH, ONE PROBLEM:
SHE'S NOT BEING RELEASED INTO CUSTODY UNTIL TOMORROW.
TELEBORIAN HASN'T EXAMINED HER YET.

THE DOCTOR SAYS YOU'RE BETTER.
YOU'LL BE TAKEN INTO CUSTODY TODAY. YOUR TRIAL DATE IS SET FOR JULY.
HAVE YOU DECIDED TO SPEAK YET?
WROTE IT.
SENT IT TO YOU.
AND YOUR BROTHER.
YOU WILL BE REMOVED FROM HERE AND TAKEN TO GÖTEBORG PRISON...
...WHERE YOU WILL BE FORMALLY CHARGED AND HELD PENDING YOUR TRIAL.
¡NO PASARAN!
POLIS

BET YOU CAN'T WAIT TO GET THE TRIAL OVER WITH, EH?
BE IN THE PRISON? AMONG ALL THOSE HOT WOMEN?
PRISON MUST BE HEAVEN FOR LESBIANS.
IS IT? IS IT HEAVEN FOR LESBIANS?
YOU WENT TO SEE NILS BJURMAN?
NO?
NOT TALKING TODAY, LISBETH?
WHAT CAN YOU TELL ME ABOUT YOUR FATHER, LISBETH?
DO YOU KNOW YOUR FATHER?
IT WOULD BE NICE IF YOU WOULD SPEAK, LISBETH.
I READ IT, LISBETH.
YOU'VE DESCRIBED EVERYTHING VERY FORCEFULLY.
STILL NOT TALKING TO ME?
Teleborian and the security services.
raped by my lawyer, the bastard Bjurman.
he STOLE my money, a disgusting rapist -

WHAT'S SO FUNNY?
LISBETH HAS SUBMITTED A WRITTEN ACCOUNT OF HER LIFE.

WOULDN'T HAVE THOUGHT THERE WAS MUCH TO LAUGH ABOUT IN THERE...
I DON'T SEE WHY THAT'S FUNNY.
MAYBE YOU'D HAVE TO KNOW HER.

"ADVOKAT GIANNINI...LET'S BE FRANK.
"YOU DO NOT HAVE ANY EXPERIENCE IN CRIMINAL LAW.
"YOU ARE A WOMEN'S RIGHTS LAWYER."

I HAVE READ THE "LIFE STORY" YOU SUBMITTED IN EVIDENCE. SHE IS CLEARLY VERY DISTURBED.
A VERY UNHAPPY YOUNG WOMAN. ARE YOU HELPING HER?
I'M TRYING MY BEST...

YOU'VE SUBMITTED A PETITION ASKING FOR HER TO BE FOUND FIT TO PLEAD.
IS SHE? BECAUSE YOU KNOW, SOMETIMES TRYING ISN'T ENOUGH...

THANKS TO MALIN ERIKSSON FOR LETTING US USE HER APARTMENT...
THE BUGGING OF THE OFFICE MEANS THAT WE HAVE TO HOLD A STAGE-MANAGED MEETING WHEN WE GET BACK THERE.
BUT WE WON'T MENTION THIS BOOK:
IT WILL ACCOMPANY A SPECIAL EDITION OF THE MAGAZINE: "THE LISBETH SALANDER STORY."
IT'S ESSENTIAL THAT THIS REMAINS SECRET *UNTIL* HER TRIAL.

Cortez, Eriksson & Blomkvist
THE SECTION
A MILLENNIUM BOOK

MIKEY, WE'RE NOT COPING WITHOUT ERIKA HERE--SHE DID SO MUCH!
I JUST CAN'T COPE WITH THE VOLUME OF WORK.

GOOD MORNING, CRISTER!
MIKEY, I DON'T KNOW WHERE HALF THE STUFF GETS FILED!
WELL, CALL ERIKA AND ASK HER, MALIN!

PUBLISHING DAG'S ***BRUTAL*** EXAMINATION OF THE SEX TRAFFICKING TRADE.
THIS WILL ACCOMPANY A SPECIAL EDITION OF THE MAGAZINE INVESTIGATING DAG'S AND MIA'S MURDERS.

WE'RE NOT COPING, ERIKA.
ME NEITHER, MALIN.
WE NEED ABOUT FOUR EXTRA MEMBERS OF STAFF.
I NEED ABOUT FORTY FEWER.
SO SORRY TO BE THE ONE TO TELL YOU THIS, ERIKA:
HOLMS HAS PUT IN A FORMAL COMPLAINT TO MANAGEMENT ABOUT YOU.
YOU COULDN'T JUST TALK TO ME!?!
WELL, I'M LISTENING NOW!
YOU DON'T FUCKING LISTEN!
YOU KILLED MY STORY!
IT WAS A GOOD STORY!
IT'S NOT "ALL ABOUT THE STORY," HOLMS.
YOUR SOURCE WAS SHIT.
PHP Parse error: parse error in dt_banner.inoon line 6
OK
HANS FASTE IS DRIP-FEEDING YOU THIS CRAP ABOUT SALANDER.
HE'S GOT AN AGENDA!

I WOULD HAVE COME HOME EARLIER.
IF YOU'D *TOLD* ME.
I HATE THIS JOB, GREGER.
I HATE THE PEOPLE AND THE ATMOSPHERE.
AGH!

PETER FREDRIKSSON.
YOU NASTY LITTLE MAN.

YOU DON'T KNOW WHAT IT WAS LIKE.
SHE WAS ALL I COULD THINK ABOUT.

BUT SHE WOULDN'T EVEN LOOK AT ME.
THE WHORE COULDN'T EVEN *FUCKING* SEE ME.

REALLY? YOU THINK THAT?
YOU'RE THE ONLY PERSON IN HUMAN HISTORY TO HEAR THE WORD "NO"?

BUT SHE.
SHUT UP.
YOU'RE TEMPTING ME TO BREAK THE OTHER KNEE.
DVD
FOR Richy FROM GREGER -CLUB X NIGHT-

ERIKA?
BORGSJÖ WANTS YOU IN HIS OFFICE.

WHAT THE ***HELL*** DO YOU CALL ***THIS?***
WHO GAVE YOU THAT?
NEVER MIND WHO GAVE IT TO ME!
PETER FREDRIKSSON STOLE IT FROM MY HOUSE.
HE GAVE IT TO YOU, DIDN'T HE?

IT'S INSULTING!
HOW CAN MILLENNIUM ***PRINT*** THIS CRAP.
THEY MUST KNOW.
NEVER KEEP YOUR JOB IF THEY DO!
THEY'VE BEEN HOLDING OFF PUBLISHING IT AS A COURTESY TO ME!
ARE YOU TRYING TO USE ME AS BARGAINING CHIP?
TO SUPPRE A STOR
THEY ***WOULDN'T DARE.***
I ***HATE*** THIS JOB.
YOU CAN SHOVE IT.

I'M LEAVING.
RIGHT NOW, FOREVER.
AND I'M APPOINTING *YOU* ACTING CHIEF EDITOR.

...I STILL HATE YOU...
THAT'S STILL MUTUAL.
BUT YOU'RE A JOURNALIST AND THERE AREN'T MANY OF THEM LEFT ANYMORE.
STILL "ALL ABOUT THE STORY"?
PUBLISH THIS ONE.
I *DARE* YOU!

THANKS FOR THIS!
THIS IS A GREAT STORY!
YEAH.
WAIT UNTIL FRISK GIVES YOU HIS INVESTIGATION INTO WHO'S BEEN FEEDING THE PRESS ANTI-SALANDER STORIES.
YOU'LL THINK IT'S CHRISTMAS.

IT'S A PATTERN THAT CAN ONLY BE IDENTIFIED OVER TIME:
MILLENNIUM EMAIL TRAFFIC IS WRONG. NO MENTION OF ZALACHENKO, EVER. NO MENTION OF NIEDERMANN. THEY SEND NO DRAFT ARTICLES TO EACH OTHER.
THEY KNOW WE'RE WATCHING?
YES.

SALANDER GOES ON TRIAL IN TWO DAYS.
WE CAN'T KNOW WHAT THEY'RE PLANNING TO PRINT, BUT IF THEY KNOW THEY'RE BEING BUGGED AND THEY'RE HIDING WHAT THEY'RE PRINTING, IT'S A SAFE GUESS THAT IT COULD LEAD TO US.
THE REAL PROBLEM IS MIKAEL BLOMKVIST'S *CREDIBILITY*.

DOES HE KNOW WE'RE BUGGING HIS APARTMENT?
NO.
WE NEED A STORY TO UNFOLD *FAR* AWAY FROM US.
WE NEED TO MAKE HIM LOOK LIKE A CONSPIRACY NUT.

COCAINE?
A **LOT** OF COCAINE. THEN THEY LEFT.
THEN **NOTHING**. NO CALLS TO THE POLICE TO SEARCH THE PLACE.

IT'S AN **INCOMPLETE** PLAY THEN. CALL THE POLICE AGAIN.
ASK IF THEY'RE BEING NUDGED INTO SEARCHING MIKAEL'S HOME.
I'M SUPPOSED TO MEET ERIKA BERGER FOR DINNER. IS IT OKAY TO GO?

I'M SURE THAT'S FINE. GIVE MONICA A NOTE OF WHERE YOU'LL BE.
AND WE'LL TO FIND OUT HAT THEY'RE PLANNING NEXT.

NO CALLS REGARDING THAT ADDRESS?
PLEASE, PHONE ME IF THE ADDRESS COMES UP, WILL YOU?

NOTHING?
NO CALLS?

SHIT!

THE NIKOS BROTHERS!
WORKED FOR ARKAN!
NYSTRÖM WAS SEEN WITH THEM TODAY.
THEY'RE GOING TO KILL MIKAEL!

YANNI'S GRE

OKAY, MONICA. ON OUR WAY.

THIS IS NICE.
OUT OF CHARACTER, BUT NICE.
I'VE NEVER BEEN MORE GLAD TO SEE YOU.

I RESIGNED.
REALLY?
I WANT TO COME BACK TO MILLENNIUM.
WELL, I DON'T KNOW IF THAT'S SAFE, RICKY!
MALIN ERIKSSON MIGHT DIE OF JOY!
GUN?!
OH GOD.
MIKEY!
DOWN!
DOWN!

BAM BAM
BAM

WHAM!

MONICA?

FUCKFUCK FUCK!

ERIKA.

THEY MUSTN'T KNOW WE GUESSED: MODIG AND ANDERSSON!

YOU WERE HAVING DINNER HERE WHEN THE GUNMAN APPEARED.

I'LL TAKE THEM TO A SAFE HOUSE UNTIL THE TRIAL IS OVER.

District Court. Stockholm.
MIKEY!
OVER HERE, BLOMKVIST!
WILL SHE SPEAK?
IS SHE GOING TO ANSWER ANY QUESTIONS AT ALL?
IS SALANDER AN ELECTIVE MUTE, MIKEY?
WELL, THAT'S A FIRST!
MIKAEL BLOMKVIST HAS NOTHING TO SAY.
MAYBE MUTENESS IS CATCHING...

YOU SEEM VERY CALM.
SHE'LL DO WELL.
I HOPE YOU'RE RIGHT ABOUT THIS, MIKEY.
IT'LL BE FINE--
IT *BETTER* BE.
PLEASE BE UPSTANDING FOR JUDGE JÖRGEN IVERSEN.
WE'RE TELLING A STORY HERE, DRAGAN.
I KNOW HOW TO TELL A STORY.
THERE'S A BIT MORE AT STAKE THAN NEWSSTAND SALES.

GOOD MORNING JOHN.
YOUR HONOR.
BRING THE ACCUSED UP, PLEASE.
YOU DID BRIEF HER ABOUT HER CLOTHES?
NO. BUT I THINK ANNIKA DID.
LISBETH SALANDER, YOU STAND CHARGED WITH COMMITTING GRIEVOUS BODILY HARM AGAINST CARL-MAGNUS LUNDIN ON THE 12TH OF APRIL THIS YEAR OUTSIDE OR NEAR THE SUMMER CABIN BELONGING TO ADVOCATE NILS BJURMAN IN THE DISTRICT OF--
CHARGE THIRTEEN FURTHER TO THE ATTEMPTED MURDER KARL AXEL BODIN CHARGED IN SUBSECT TWO ABOVE, THAT W IN POSSESSION OF ILLEGAL WEAPON, SPECIFICALLY--

PROSECUTING COUNSEL: OPENING STATEMENTS?
YES, YOUR HONOR.
THESE CHARGES AGAINST LISBETH SALANDER.
THEY DO NOT ARISE FROM AN EXTRAORDINARY SET OF CIRCUM-STANCES.
THEY ARE PART OF AN ONGOING PATTERN IN THIS POOR WOMAN'S CHAOTIC LIFE.
THESE SIXTEEN CHARGES ARE THE TIP OF THE ICEBERG.
THIS POOR CREATURE HAS SUFFERED FROM MENTAL HEALTH PROBLEMS ALL HER LIFE.

HOSPITALIZED SINCE THE AGE OF TWELVE...
...FOR ATTEMPTING TO BURN HER FATHER TO DEATH, UNTIL THE PRESENT DAY--
--LISBETH SALANDER HAS SUFFERED FROM DELUSIONS--
THAT MAKE HER BOTH VIOLENT AND YET, AT THE SAME TIME--
--INCAPABLE OF BEING HELD TO ACCOUNT FOR HER ACTIONS.
SHE HAS NOT SPOKEN ONE WORD TO THE POLICE. IT IS NOT KNOWN WHETHER SHE SPOKE TO HER DEFENSE TEAM.
MY COLLEAGUE, ADVOKAT GIANNINI, THOUGH A WELL-KNOWN CIVIL RIGHTS LAWYER...
...IS UNFAMILIAR WITH CRIMINAL LAW.
SHE IS PERHAPS UNAWARE THAT BOTH MENTAL INTENT AND THE PHYSICAL ACTION OF ANY CRIMINAL CHARGE MUST BE PROVED.

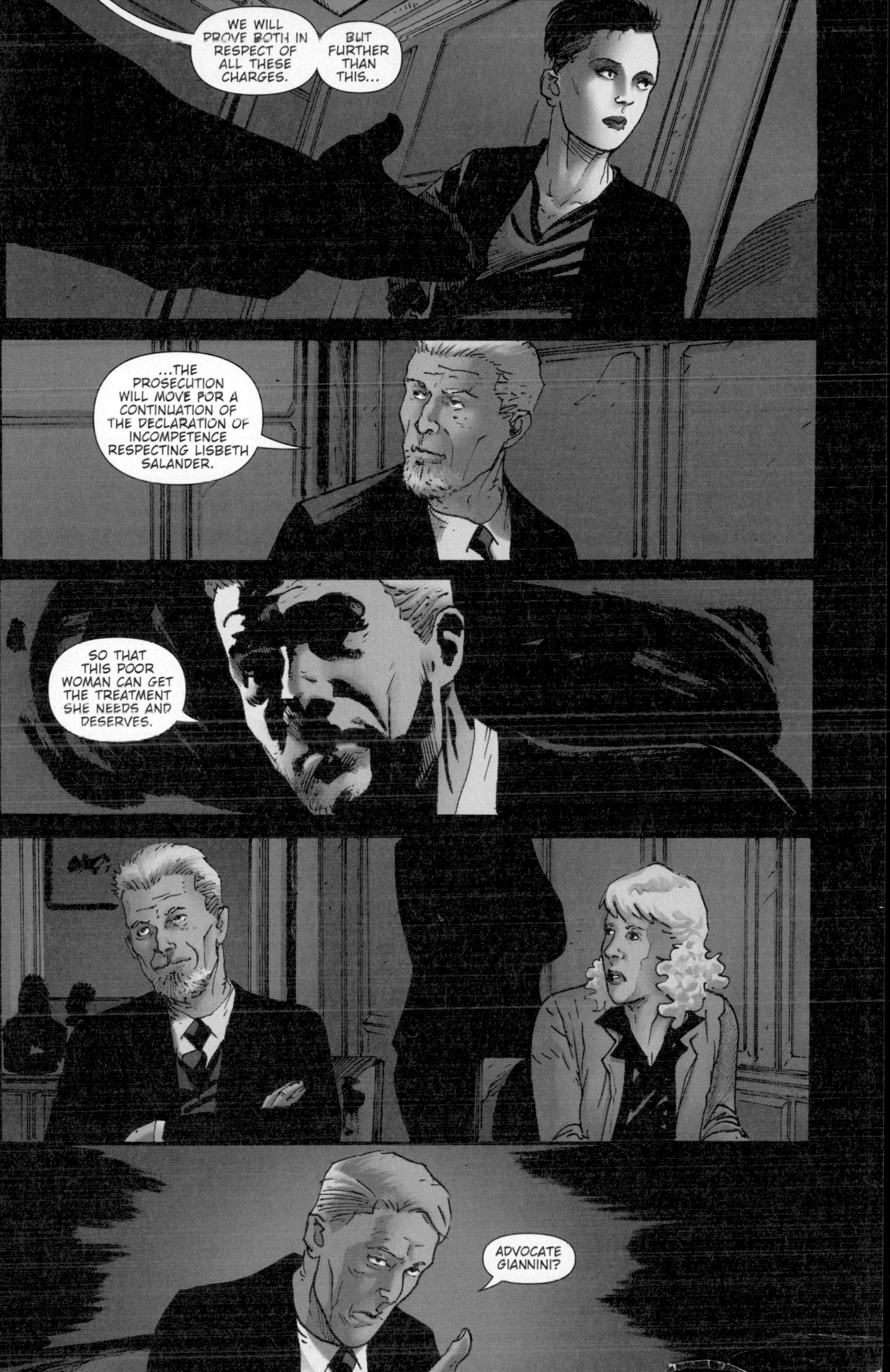
WE WILL PROVE BOTH IN RESPECT OF ALL THESE CHARGES.
BUT FURTHER THAN THIS...
...THE PROSECUTION WILL MOVE FOR A CONTINUATION OF THE DECLARATION OF INCOMPETENCE RESPECTING LISBETH SALANDER.
SO THAT THIS POOR WOMAN CAN GET THE TREATMENT SHE NEEDS AND DESERVES.
ADVOCATE GIANNINI?

YES, HELLO?
WOULD YOU LIKE TO MAKE OPENING STATEMENTS?
MY CLIENT ADMITS TO OWNING A CAN OF MACE.
OTHERWISE, WE DEMAND ACQUITTAL ON ALL CHARGES.
AND THAT HER CURRENT DECLARATION OF INCOMPETENCE BE REVOKED.
IS THAT ALL YOU WANT TO SAY, ADVOKAT GIANNINI?
YEAH.

ARE YOU SURE?
YES.
I'D LIKE TO SEE BOTH OF YOU IN MY CHAMBERS RIGHT NOW, PLEASE.
--ABSOLUTELY ESSENTIAL THAT THE CASE IS HEARD IN CAMERA.
YOU'D BETTER HAVE VERY GOOD REASONS:
THE PRESS WILL HATE BEING EXCLUDED.
ESPECIALLY SINCE YOU'VE BEEN SO OPEN WITH THEM RECENTLY.
...?
IT'S STOCKHOLM, EKSTRÖM.
I KNOW YOU'VE BEEN BRIEFING JOURNALISTS THAT SHE'S A MUTE.
WELL, THE BASIS FOR ASKING FOR A CLOSED COURT IS THE NATIONAL SECURITY THREAT.
AS WELL AS SALANDER'S FRAGILE MENTAL HEALTH.

KARL AXEL BODIN WAS A KGB AGENT WHO DEFECTED.
THE NATIONAL SECURITY IMPLICATIONS OF AN OPEN COURT ARE *IMMEASURABLE* AT THIS POINT.
I MEAN, SHE PROBABLY WON'T SPEAK ANYWAY.
HAVE YOU ANYTHING TO ADD TO THIS?
NO.
QUITE HAPPY FOR THE CASE TO TAKE PLACE BEHIND CLOSED DOORS?
YEAH.
I'M GOING TO GRANT THIS MOTION.
BUT IF I GET A SNIFF THAT YOU ARE BRIEFING THE PRESS. I'LL DEMAND YOUR REMOVAL, EKSTRÖM,
UNDERSTOOD?
THE CASE WILL BE HEARD IN CAMERA.
CLEAR THE PUBLIC BENCHES.
I DIDN'T FORESEE THAT.
COFFEE?

"WON'T IT WORRY YOU?"
"WHAT?"
"GIVING EVIDENCE IN COURT WHEN YOU HAVEN'T BEEN FOLLOWING PROCEEDINGS?"
ANNIKA KNOWS WHAT SHE'S DOING.
YOU SAID IT WAS ALL ABOUT THE WAY THE STORY WAS TOLD.
IT *IS*.
BUT *YOU'RE* THE STORY-TELLER, MIKEY.
NOT ANNIKA.
IF SHE GETS IT WRONG LISBETH IS GOING TO BE IMPRISONED FOR THE REST OF HER LIFE.
AND SHE HASN'T MADE THE BEST START!
D'YOU THINK SO?
I THOUGHT SHE HANDLED IT QUITE WELL.

"MISS SALANDER.
"LET ME BEGIN WITH THE FIRST CHARGE..."
YOU DRIVING TO NILS BJURMAN'S SUMMER CABIN AND SHOOTING CARL-MAGNUS LUNDIN IN THE FOOT.

MISS SALANDER?
ARE WE TO ASSUME THAT YOU ARE NOT GOING TO ANSWER?
ANSWER WHAT?
WELL, PROSECUTOR EKSTRÖM'S QUESTION.
HE HASN'T ASKED ONE.
"YOU DRIVING TO NILS BJURMAN'S SUMMER CABIN AND SHOOTING CARL-MAGNUS LUNDIN IN THE FOOT"--
THAT IS NOT A QUESTION.
IT'S AN ASSERTION OF REFUTABLE *FACT*.
BUT IT'S NOT A QUESTION.
IF HE ASKS ME A QUESTION I'LL ANSWER A QUESTION.

DID YOU DRIVE TO BJURMAN'S CABIN AND SHOOT LUNDIN?
NO.
YOU *DIDN'T* SHOOT HIM?
I DIDN'T DRIVE.
I TOOK THE TRAIN.
BUT YOU *WERE* THERE?
YES.
AND THEN THEY SHOWED UP?
YES.
WHY WERE THEY THERE?
I DUNNO.
WHAT DID YOU THINK AT THE TIME?
I ASSUMED THEY WANTED TO BURN THE PLACE DOWN.
THEY HAD A CAN OF PETROL WITH THEM.
WHY WERE *YOU* THERE?

LOOKING FOR INFORMATION ABOUT THE BASTARD'S MURDER.
"BASTARD"?!
WHO DO YOU MEAN BY "BASTARD"?
NILS BJURMAN?
YES.
WHY WOULD YOU CALL HIM THAT?
BECAUSE HE WAS A BASTARD.
IN WHAT WAY?
HE WAS A RAPIST.
ARE YOU SAYING HE *RAPED* YOU?

WHEN DID THIS "RAPE" OCCUR?
YES.
TUESDAY THE 18TH OF FEBRUARY 2003 BETWEEN 7 AND 9.
THE SECOND TIME WAS FRIDAY MARCH THE 7TH OF THE SAME YEAR.
VERY PRECISE, THANK YOU.
YES, THANK YOU FOR THAT...
AND YET, I NOTE THAT YOU HAVE REFUSED TO DISCUSS THIS WITH THE POLICE?
THEY HAVE TRIED TIME AND AGAIN...
...TO GET INFORMATION FROM YOU ABOUT THIS "ASSERTION OF REFUTABLE FACT."
YET YOU REFUSE TO TALK TO THEM?
I WROTE ABOUT IT IN MY AUTOBIOGRAPHICAL STATEMENT.
YES, SO YOU DID. YOU KNOW WHY THE POLICE LIKE TO TALK TO PEOPLE ABOUT "ASSERTIONS OF REFUTABLE FACT" SO THAT THEY CAN QUESTION THEM?
GET THE OTHER POINT OF VIEW, DO YOU SEE?

SO THAT IF I SAY YOU PUNCHED ME, FOR EXAMPLE, AND THE POLICE CAN QUESTION ME ABOUT IT...
THEY MIGHT SAY, "BUT LISBETH WAS IN PRISON AT THAT TIME" OR "LISBETH WAS AT WORK."
DO YOU SEE?
THAT'S WHY WE DON'T ALL JUST WRITE AUTOBIOGRAPHICAL STATEMENTS, LISBETH.
SO THAT THE REALITY OF OUR "ASSERTIONS OF REFUTABLE FACTS" CAN BE TESTED.
DID YOU REPORT THE RAPE TO A FRIEND?
NO.
A LAWYER?
NO.
A DOCTOR OR RAPE CRISIS CENTER?
NO.
THE POLICE?
NO, I DON'T TRUST THEM.
THERE IS NOTHING IN HIS PAST TO SUPPORT THAT.
NILS BJURMAN WAS AN UPSTANDING MEMBER OF THE LEGAL COMMUNITY FOR TWENTY-THREE YEARS BEFORE HE WAS MURDERED.

BASICALLY, THERE'S ONLY YOUR WORD AGAINST HIS--
HE'S DEAD.
AND YOU HAVE A LONG HISTORY OF PARANOID SCHIZOPHRENIA.
ANYTHING TO ADD? NO QUESTIONS?
NO.
SENIOR ADMINISTRATIVE OFFICER AT THE GUARDIANSHIP AGENCY FOR THE PAST TWENTY YEARS?
YES.
AND IN YOUR CAPACITY THERE...
HAVE YOU EVER RECEIVED A COMPLAINT ABOUT NILS BJURMAN?
NOT ONE.
IN TWENTY YEARS.
HE WAS A LOVELY MAN.
HE WORKED VERY HARD FOR HIS CLIENTS.
HE DIDN'T DESERVE THAT...

ADVOKAT GIANNINI HAS MOVED FOR SALANDER'S DECLARATION OF INCOMPETENCE TO BE RESCINDED IMMEDIATELY.
IN YOUR PROFESSIONAL OPINION, WOULD THAT BE WISE?
FOR IT TO BE RESCINDED, MISS SALANDER WOULD HAVE TO SUBMIT HERSELF FOR A PSYCHIATRIC ASSESSMENT.
BUT SHE FLATLY REFUSES TO DO SO.
WERE YOU IN NILS BJURMAN'S APARTMENT ON THE 7TH TO THE 8TH OF MARCH 2003?
NO, I WAS NOT.
YOU DON'T KNOW WHAT HAPPENED THEN, DO YOU?
NO. I CAN'T IN GOOD CONSCIENCE SAY I DO.

STATE YOUR NAME, PLEASE.
I AM MELKER HANSSON.
AND YOUR SPECIALTY, PLEASE.
FORENSIC SPECIALIST.
AND YOUR AREA OF EXPERTISE, PLEASE.
FORENSIC RECONSTRUCTION.
I TAKE FORENSIC CIRCUMSTANCES...
...AND RECONSTRUCT THE MOVEMENT OF THE PARTICIPANTS IN THOSE EVENTS.
...AS WE SEE HERE: LISBETH SALANDER'S BLOOD ACTUALLY IN AND AROUND THE OPEN GRAVE FOUND AT A DEPTH OF APPROXIMATELY 985 CM TO 95 CM.
THIS TENDS US TOWARDS THE CONCLUSION THAT SHE WAS *IN* THE RECENTLY DUG GRAVE *POST* INJURY.
AND FROM THE PATTERN OF BLEEDING ON THE GRAVE FLOOR WE CAN TRACE THE HIP, HEAD AND SHOULDER BLEEDS SHE WAS SUBSEQUENTLY TREATED FOR.

...INFRARED.
WE CAN TRACE THE MOVEMENT OF THE WEAPONS AROUND THE GOSSEBERGA FARM AREA.
AND FROM THIS CAN WE CONCLUDE THAT SHE INTENDED TO KILL HER FATHER?
NO.
WHAT DO YOU MEAN, NO?
WE CAN'T DRAW ANY CONCLUSIONS LIKE THAT.
IN OUR PRE-TRIAL INTERVIEWS, DIDN'T YOU SAY THAT WE MIGHT DRAW THAT CONCLUSION?
NO. YOU SAID THAT. I DIDN'T GET A CHANCE TO TALK.
ONE CAN'T SCIENTIFICALLY INFER INTENT FROM MOVE-MENTS.
ANYTHING TO ADD?
NO.
NO QUESTIONS?
NO.

I HAVEN'T BEEN OUT IN THE FIELD FOR A LONG TIME.

MAYBE YOU SHOULD STAY IN THE CAR?

"BIRGER WADENSJÖÖ, I'M TORSTEN EDKLINTH OF THE CONSTITUTION PROTECTION UNIT WITH SÄPO...
"...AND I'M HEREBY AUTHORIZED BY THE PROSECUTOR GENERAL TO ARREST YOU FOR MURDER OF GUNNAR BJÖRCK."
POLI
BJÖRCK?!
YOU WILL FURTHER BE CHARGED WITH A SERIES OF OFFENSES RELATING TO BREACHES OF THE CONSTITUTIONAL RIGHTS OF A NUMBER OF CITIZENS DURING THE COURSE OF YOUR HANDLING OF THE ZALACHENKO CASE--
CLINTON! IT WAS ALL CLINTON'S IDEA!
COME AND TALK TO US...
WE'RE ALL EARS.

POLIS
EVERT GULLBERG CAME BACK--
--THE FOUNDER AND RETIRED HEAD OF THE ZALA UNIT?
--AND HE CALLED IN FREDRIK CLINTON.
THE MAN YOU'D TAKEOVER FROM?
EXACTLY.
I WAS NOT A "WAR TIME" LEADER.
APPARENTLY.
I DID MY BEST,
BUT I WOULD NEVER HAVE CHOSEN THE SOLUTIONS GULLBERG DID.
YOU KNEW NOTHING ABOUT IT?
THE FIRST THING I KNEW ABOUT THE PLAN TO KILL ZALA WAS WHEN I HEARD ABOUT IT ON TV.
TELL ME ABOUT GUNNAR BJÖRCK'S "SUICIDE."
"SUICIDE"?

DON'T BE CAREFUL WITH ME, WADENSJÖÖ. IT WAS SO BADLY STAGED.
BJÖRCK TRASHED HIS HOUSE AND THEN HANGED HIMSELF FROM A NOOSE...
THAT HE COULDN'T REACH ON HIS OWN?
OKAY.
CLINTON WANTED SOMEONE TO SILENCE BJÖRCK.
NYSTRÖM CHOSE TWO SERBS--
--TOMI AND MIRO NIKOLICH--
IDIOTS.
GUN-HAPPY.
UNPROFESSIONAL.
INCOMPETENT.
IDIOTS!
THAT WILL HAPPEN IF YOU RECRUIT FROM THE SERBIAN MAFIA.
IT WASN'T ME.
I DIDN'T RECRUIT THEM.
IN THIS MAELSTROM OF ILLEGALITY AND STATE-SPONSORED VIOLENCE...
YOU DID NOTHING. ABSOLUTELY NOTHING.
WELL DONE.
GIVE ME DETAILS: ALL SURVEILLANCE, ALL OPERATIONS.
EVERY MOVE YOUR UNIT HAS MADE.
LEAVE OUT ONE DETAIL...
AND I'LL SEE THAT YOU NEVER GET OUT OF PRISON.

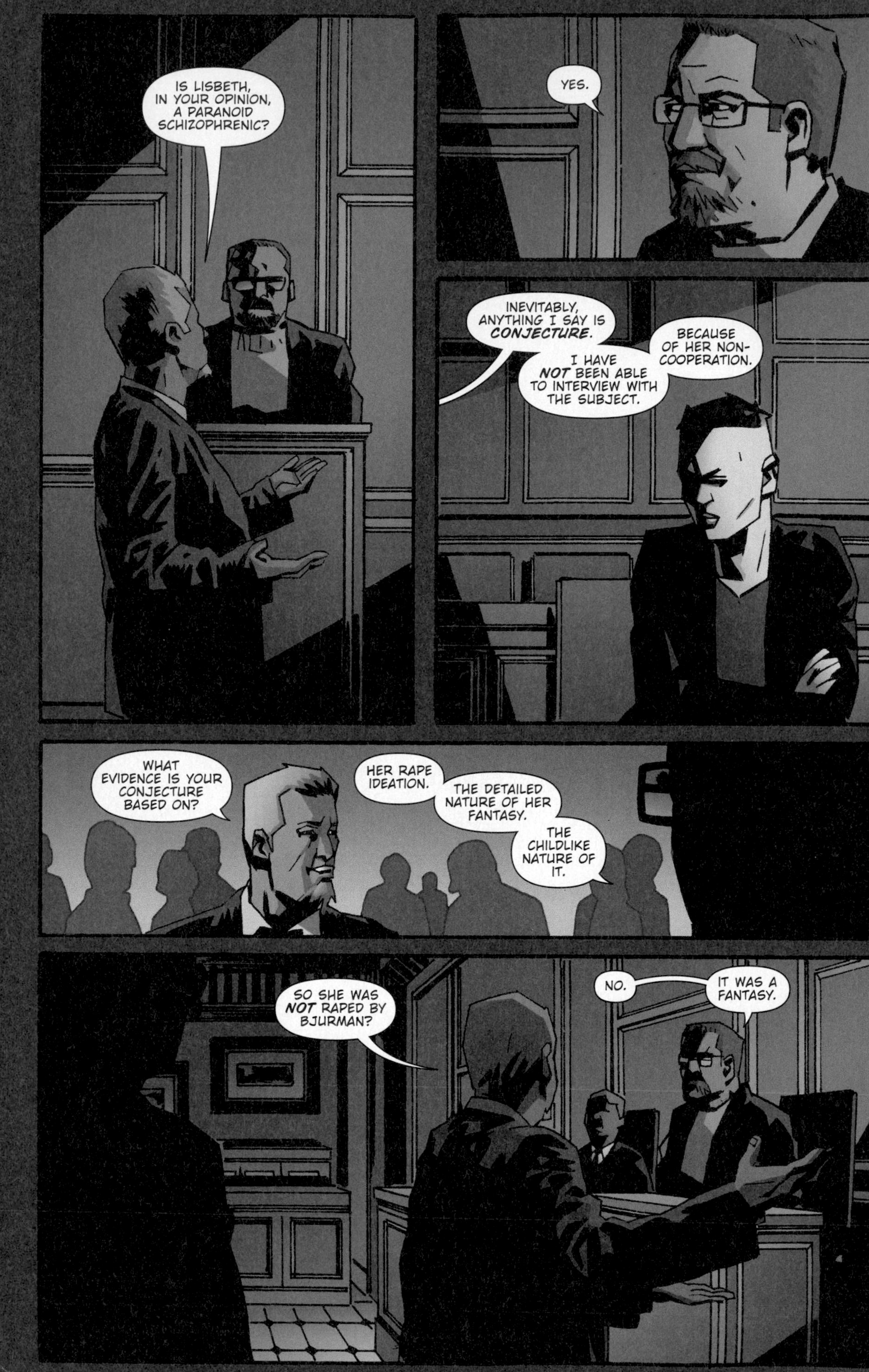

IS LISBETH, IN YOUR OPINION, A PARANOID SCHIZOPHRENIC?
YES.
INEVITABLY, ANYTHING I SAY IS **CONJECTURE**.
I HAVE **NOT** BEEN ABLE TO INTERVIEW WITH THE SUBJECT.
BECAUSE OF HER NON-COOPERATION.
WHAT EVIDENCE IS YOUR CONJECTURE BASED ON?
HER RAPE IDEATION.
THE DETAILED NATURE OF HER FANTASY.
THE CHILDLIKE NATURE OF IT.
SO SHE WAS **NOT** RAPED BY BJURMAN?
NO.
IT WAS A FANTASY.

NOW YOU FEATURE IN HER AUTOBIOGRAPHICAL ESSAY.
YES, I DO.
QUITE HEAVILY IN FACT.
SHE CLAIMS SHE WAS ABUSED BY BEING HELD IN RESTRAINTS.
THAT I VISITED HER ROOM LATE AT NIGHT, ALONE.
CLASSIC MANIFESTATION.
AND THIS LEADS YOU TO CONCLUDE THAT SHE'S PARANOID SCHIZOPHRENIC?
IT DOES INDEED.
NO FURTHER QUESTIONS.
ANY QUESTIONS?
QUITE A LOT ACTUALLY.
COULD WE STOP FOR AN EARLY LUNCH?
THEN RUN STRAIGHT THROUGH?
VERY WELL.

MASTER AN S
GEORG NYSTRÖM--
YOU ARE UNDER ARREST...
ON SUSPICION OF BEING AN ACCESSORY TO MURDER AND ATTEMPTED MURDER.
YOU DON'T KNOW WHO WE ARE...
YES WE DO, NYSTRÖM.
WE KNOW EXACTLY WHO YOU ARE.

POLIS
BIP
WELCOME TO THE INNER SANCTUM OF THE STATE SECURITY SERVICE.
CHIEF OF SECRETARIAT ALBERT SHENKE.
YOU ARE UNDER ARREST FOR VIOLATION OF THE SWEDISH CONSTITUTION.
THIS IS AN OUTRAGE!

LET NO ONE IN.
IF ANYONE *TRIES,* I AUTHORIZE YOU TO DRAW YOUR REVOLVERS.
READY?
INDEED.

CHIEF OF BUDGET GUSTAV ATTERBOM.
WE ARE ARRESTING YOU FOR VIOLATION OF THE SWEDISH CONSTITUTION.

HOW DARE YOU!
THIS IS OUTRAGEOUS!
MY LIFE HAS BEEN SPENT IN SERVICE TO MY COUNTRY!

YOU FINANCED PHONE TAPPING, MURDER, PEOPLE TRAFFICKING, THE INCARCERATION AND TORTURE OF A CHILD IN A STATE PSYCHIATRIC INSTITUTION.
YOU'RE QUITE RIGHT.
IT *IS* AN OUTRAGE.

POLICE!
OPEN UP!
POLIS
POLIS

WHAT'S GOING ON?
WE'RE THE POLICE!
SO AM I!

WE'RE HERE TO ARREST YOU FOR PHONE TAPPING.
BREAKING AND ENTERING MIKAEL BLOMKVIST'S' FLAT.
PLANTING EVIDENCE AND POSSESSION OF COCAINE.

LOOK, YOU DON'T GET IT: *I'M A POLICEMAN.*

NO, *YOU* DON'T GET IT.
THOSE DAYS ARE OVER.

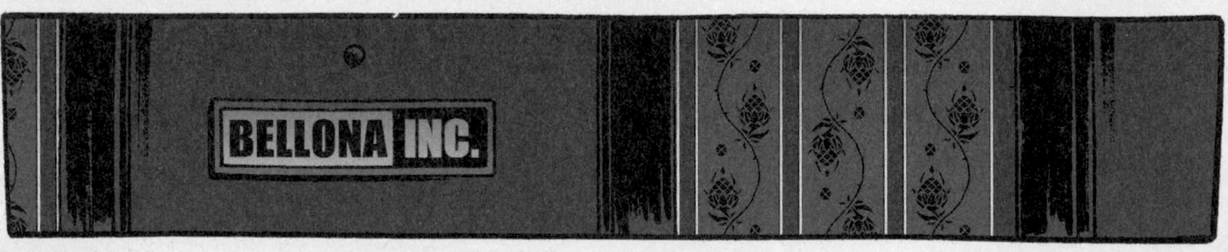
BELLONA INC.

LONA INC.

WHA--?

...ACCESSORY TO THE MURDERS OF GUNNAR BJÖRCK AND ALEXANDER ZALACHENKO.
ALSO AS AN ACCOMPLICE TO THE ATTEMPTED MURDERS OF MIKAEL BLOMKVIST AND ERIKA BERGER.
PUT YOUR TROUSERS ON.
YOU'RE COMING WITH US.
YOU'RE JOKING.
FREDRIK CLINTON?
THAT'S ME.
OH MY GOD.

YOU MAY SIT DOWN.
DR. TELEBORIAN, CAN YOU TELL ME WHY YOU SAID LISBETH'S RAPE ALLEGATIONS AGAINST BJURMAN ARE FALSE?
AN AUTHORITY FIGURE ATTACKED HER WHEN NO ONE WAS LOOKING!
THERE IS NO EVIDENCE.
SHE TOLD NO ONE.
IT'S OBVIOUSLY FABRICATED.
WE'RE ABOUT TO PROVE THAT SHE IS SANE.
THAT EVERYTHING SHE SAYS IS TRUE.
DR. TELEBORIAN ASSERTS THAT SHE MAKES ALLEGATIONS BECAUSE SHE IS MAD.
AND THE PROOF THAT SHE IS MAD IS THIS: THAT SHE MAKES ALLEGA-TIONS.
THAT HER RIGHTS HAVE BEEN BREACHED OVER AND OVER AGAIN.
AND THAT DR. TELEBORIAN IS A FALSE WITNESS.

LISBETH CLAIMS SHE SPENT 380 DAYS IN FULL RESTRAINTS.
DURING HER 786 DAYS UNDER YOUR CARE IN ST. STEPHAN'S.
NONSENSE.
IT WAS NO MORE THAN 30.
WHAT WOULD YOU SAY IF IT WAS 380?
WELL, OBVIOUSLY THAT IS GROTESQUELY EXCESSIVE.
FULL PHYSICAL RESTRAINTS SHOULD ONLY BE USED IN THE MOST EXCEPTIONAL CIRCUMSTANCES.
IT MIGHT HELP TO CLEAR THIS UP.
IF WE COULD REFER TO THE MEDICAL RECORD.
CAN YOU DESCRIBE "FULL PHYSICAL RESTRAINTS"?
WELL, THE PATIENT WOULD BE HELD BY STRAPS ON THEIR ARMS AND ANKLES TO A BED.
THEY CAN'T EVEN SCRATCH THEIR NOSE?
IT'S FOR THEIR OWN SAFETY.
BUT OBVIOUSLY, THOSE ARE *CLASSIFIED*.
SALANDER DOSSIER
IT SAYS IN HER MEDICAL RECORD THAT SHE WAS HELD LIKE THAT FOR 381 DAYS, OUT OF A TOTAL OF 786.

HOW CAN YOU HAVE THEM?
WHERE DID YOU GET THEM?
YOU SHOWED THIS RECORD TO PROSECUTOR EKSTRÖM.
DIDN'T YOU?
BUT I DIDN'T MEAN--
YOU BROKE THE CLASSIFIED STATUS UNDER CRIMINAL LAW. UNDER THE RULES OF DISCOVERY.
THE PROSECUTION CANNOT HAVE ACCESS TO INFORMATION AND THEN DENY ACCESS TO THE DEFENSE.
SO YOU ARE PROVABLY WRONG ABOUT THAT.
AREN'T YOU?
DR. TELEBORIAN?
IN SOME WAYS...
I MAY HAVE UNDER-ESTIMATED...
THAT IS THE FIRST THING YOU'VE SAID THAT I WOULDN'T DISPUTE.

YOU SAY SHE'S A "DANGER TO HERSELF."
HAS LISBETH EVER TRIED TO SELF HARM?
LOOK AT HER. SHE'S GOT TATTOOS EVERYWHERE.
IT'S OBVIOUS EVIDENCE OF SELF-HATE.
I HAVE A TATTOO.
DO YOU?
JUST A LITTLE ONE.
IT WOULD BE INAPPROPRIATE TO SHOW YOU..
I'M NOT PATHOLOGIZING TATTOOS PER SE.
BUT HERS ARE EXCESSIVE.
WHAT PERCENTAGE OF BODY COVERAGE MAKES TATTOOING CLINICALLY SIGNIFICANT?
THAT'S A SILLY QUESTION.
IS IT?
ISN'T SHE JUST EXPRESSING A SOCIAL IDENTITY?
ASSERTING HER MEMBERSHIP OF A SOCIAL SUBCULTURE?

YOU STARTED RESTRAINING HER WHEN SHE WAS THIRTEEN, IS THAT RIGHT?
THAT IS THE AGE SHE CAME UNDER MY CARE, YES.
DID SHE HAVE TATTOOS THEN?
YOU SIMPLY DON'T UNDERSTAND THE CLINICAL REASONING.
SHE WAS A DANGER TO *HERSELF*.
SHE TRIED TO STARVE HERSELF TO *DEATH*.
IS THAT TRUE, LISBETH?
I REFUSED TO EAT.
FOR WEEKS AT A TIME?
YES. HE WAS PUTTING DRUGS IN MY FOOD.
HOW DID YOU SURVIVE?
TWO NURSES SMUGGLED IN SANDWICHES FOR ME.
THEY SAW ME WASTING AWAY. THEY KNEW WHY I WOULDN'T EAT.
IS IT NOT TRUE THAT MEMBERS OF STAFF COMPLAINED...
BOTH FORMALLY, AND INFORMALLY, ABOUT YOUR TREATMENT, LISBETH?

LOOK! I'M THE DOCTOR HERE. YOU DON'T KNOW ANYTHING ABOUT--

WRONG AGAIN, DR. TELEBORIAN.

I AM A FULLY TRAINED CLINICAL PSYCHOLOGIST.

DR. CALDIN, YOUR SUPERIOR AT THE TIME, VIGOROUSLY DISPUTED YOUR TREATMENT OF LISBETH.

UNFORTUNATELY DR. CALDIN IS NOW DEAD.

BUT HOLGER PALMGREN WORKED WITH HIM.

WOULD YOU MIND READING FROM YOUR CLINICAL NOTES AT THE TIME?

"HIS TREATMENT OF HER IS CLINICALLY BAFFLING."

"AMOUNTING TO TORTURE."

"WE MUST FIND A WAY TO REMOVE HER FROM HIS CARE."

AND DID YOU FIND A WAY?

WE MANAGED TO MOVE FOR FOSTERING AND DR. CALDIN MOVED HEAVEN AND EARTH--

--TO ENSURE I BECAME HER LEGAL GUARDIAN.

YOU REFER CONSISTENTLY TO HER "RAPE FANTASIES."

IT IS ONE OF THE FEATURES OF HER CONDITION.

SHE ACCUSED NILS BJURMAN, MYSELF--ANYONE AND EVERYONE--OF INAPPROPRIATE BEHAVIOR.

IT IS THE ONLY POWER SHE HAS.

SADLY, I THINK SHE MAY BELIEVE IT TO BE TRUE.

ARE YOU READY, LISBETH?

YES.

WHEN WAS THIS FILM MADE?
7TH MARCH 2003.
WITH A CAMERA HIDDEN IN MY RUCKSACK.
YOU GIRLS.
"ONE OF THE FEATURES OF HER CONDITION."
YOU USED THAT PHRASE IN YOUR ASSESSMENT.
CAN YOU READ THE DATE ON THE ASSESSMENT FOR ME, PLEASE?
CLICK
17TH OF MAY.
THE PRISON LOG SAYS YOU BEGAN YOUR EXAMINATION ON THE 19TH. ARE YOU PSYCHIC?
THE DATES ARE MADE UP! SOMEONE HAS CHANGED THE DATE TO DISCREDIT ME!
IT WAS RECEIVED AND LOGGED ON THE 17TH OF MAY...
...BY THE CONSTITUTIONAL PROTECTION UNIT OF THE SECURITY POLICE.
IF THE COURT WILLS, I CAN CALL WITNESSES TO CONFIRM THIS.
DOES PROSECUTOR EKSTRÖM REQUIRE THAT?
I DON'T THINK THAT WILL BE NECESSARY.

I DON'T HAVE ANY FURTHER QUESTIONS FOR THIS WITNESS.
DR. TELEBORIAN? I'M AFRAID YOU CANNOT LEAVE UNDER YOUR OWN RECOGNIZANCE.
THE POLICE HAVE ADVISED US THAT THEY WANT TO TALK TO YOU. IT'S ABOUT THE CONTENTS OF YOUR HARD DRIVE.
HOW DID YOU GET INTO MY HARD DRIVE?
THIS IS A BREACH OF MY RIGHT TO PRIVACY!
CAN WE MOVE NOW TO THE SUMMING UP? PERHAPS YOU COULD GO FIRST, ADVOKAT GIANNINI?
LISBETH SALANDER HAS HAD HER RIGHTS UNDERMINED BY THIS STATE TO PROTECT ITS OWN INTEREST IN THE SPY ZALACHENKO.
THROUGH MORAL COMPROMISE, ACTIVE PERSECUTION, CRIMES OF SEXUAL VIOLENCE, DENYING HER AGENCY.
AND THEN WE ARE SHOCKED THAT SHE DOESN'T TRUST US. SHOCKED SHE WILL NOT GO TO THE POLICE, SHOCKED SHE SEEKS TO PROTECT HERSELF.
IT IS HYPOCRISY OF THE WORST KIND: A BRUTAL, SANCTIMONIOUS, VICIOUS CAMPAIGN AGAINST A CHILD.
THE OPERATIVES RESPONSIBLE FOR THESE ACTIONS HAVE ALL BEEN ARRESTED TODAY.
I MOVE THAT THE DECLARATION OF INCOMPETENCE BE RESCINDED AND LISBETH SALANDER, FINALLY, BE GRANTED HER FREEDOM.

I ACCEPT THAT MOTION AND MOVE TO HAVE THE CHARGES DISMISSED.
FURTHER, I WOULD LIKE TO GIVE EVIDENCE TO THE COURT OF ATTEMPTS TO MANIPULATE *THIS* PROSECUTOR THROUGH THE PRESENTATION OF FORGED EVIDENCE.
WELL, THAT'LL BE VERY INTERESTING, PROSECUTOR EKSTRÖM. I'LL LOOK FORWARD TO THAT...
...BUT PERHAPS WE COULD DEAL WITH MISS SALANDER'S PREDICAMENT FIRST?
YOU ARE FREE TO GO, MISS SALANDER.
THIS CASE IS NOT ABOUT SPIES.
IT'S ABOUT VIOLENCE AGAINST WOMEN.
AND THE MEN WHO ENABLE I AND COVE IT UP.
LISBETH.
news
PICK UP? LISBETH?
GLAD TO BE BACK, RICKY?
GLAD TO BE BACK! GLAD SHE WON!
GLAD TO SEE MY OLDEST FRIEND SO HAPPY!
I'M IN LOVE WITH HER.

LISBETH?
IS THAT YOU? I'M IN PARIS, BABY.
WITH MY MUM. BUT I'LL COME HOME FOR YOU...
I'LL COME HOME SOON...

JUST ARRIVED YESTERDAY.

YEAH.

Agneta Sofia Salander

SCHWEIZERISCHE N BANK

KLUNG
HELLO, LITTLE SISTER.

NIEDERMANN.
WHAT HAPPENED TO YOUR HAND?
THE CUT YOU GAVE ME GOT INFECTED.
I HAD TO CUT IT OFF.
NICE PLACE.
YOU DIDN'T THINK TO LEAVE SWEDEN?
TRIED. COULDN'T GET OUT. ALL THE PORTS AND BORDERS HAD PICTURES OF ME.
YOU WOULDN'T MISTAKE ME FOR ANYONE ELSE, WOULD YOU?
I KNEW THERE WAS FOOD HERE.
A BED AND STUFF. THEN I GOT ILL.
FOOD?
WE USED TO PEOPLE-SMUGGLE HERE.
WOMEN. FROM RUSSIA. KEPT THEM HERE.
IS THAT WHO'S SWIMMING DOWN-STAIRS?

I FORGOT THEY WERE HERE. WHEN I CAME BACK AND FOUND THEM, THEY WERE DEAD IN THE STORAGE CONTAINER.
WELL, NEARLY. I GAVE THEM A LITTLE HELP AT THE END. THE LOOSE ENDS...
THINGS YOU FORGET...
I EVEN FORGOT ABOUT *YOU* SOME-TIMES....
KRASH

PAPPAP

YOU FUCKING BITCH!

YOU FUCKING BITCH....
TUNK
YOU FUCKING BITCH!

RAMM
DON'T LIKE ANONYMOUS TIP-OFFS. KEEP YOUR EYES OPEN.
WE WANT THAT FUCKER NIEDERMANN *DEAD* AND OUR FUCKING MONEY BACK.
POLIS
BRING BRING BRING
HI, POLICE?
YES, I'VE JUST SEEN SOME VERY HEAVILY ARMED MEN MARCHING INTO A DERELICT BUILDING...
THEY LOOK LIKE A BIKER GANG.

BRING
BRING

HI.
WHAT?
RONALD NIEDERMANN IS DEAD.
THE SVAVELSJÖ M.C. FOUND HIM IN A DERELICT FACTORY.
THEY KILLED HIM BEFORE THE POLICE ARRIVED.
SONNY NIEMINEN WAS KILLED IN THE SHOOTOUT THAT FOLLOWED.
THOUGHT YOU MIGHT BE INTERESTED...
WHAT'S THAT?
BAGELS.
I REMEMBERED YOU LIKE THEM.
YEAH. I'LL HAVE THEM.

CAN'T WE BE FRIENDS, LISBETH?
I KIND OF MISS YOU.
FRIENDS?
YEAH, FRIENDS.
I DON'T KNOW WHAT THAT MEANS.

WELL, WE DON'T FUCK.
WE JUST DRINK COFFEE, EAT BAGELS, HANG OUT.
IF YOU WANT FRIENDS...
DO YOU *LIKE* THE IDEA OF HAVING FRIENDS?
DON'T KNOW YET.
BUT I DO LIKE BAGELS.
THE END

GMM

ERLANDER

GALLERY

Character sketches by Andrea Mutti

Character sketches by Andrea Mutti

Opposite: Cover art by Lee Bermejo

THE GIRL WHO KICKED THE HORNETS' NEST

DENISE MINA is a Scottish crime writer and playwright. Her first novel, Garnethill, won the Crime Writers' Association John Creasey Dagger for the best first crime novel. She is also known for writing the DC Comics series Hellblazer and the graphic novel A Sickness in the Family.

ANDREA MUTTI attended the International School of Comics in Brescia. He has worked extensively for the French market and is known for his work on the Vertigo series DMZ and The Executor.

ANTONIO FUSO is a comic book artist and illustrator known for his sharp and frenetic style. Works include the Vertigo graphic novel A SICKNESS IN THE FAMILY (with Denise Mina) and G.I. Joe: Cobra. He lives and works in Rome, Italy, and is addicted to caffeine.

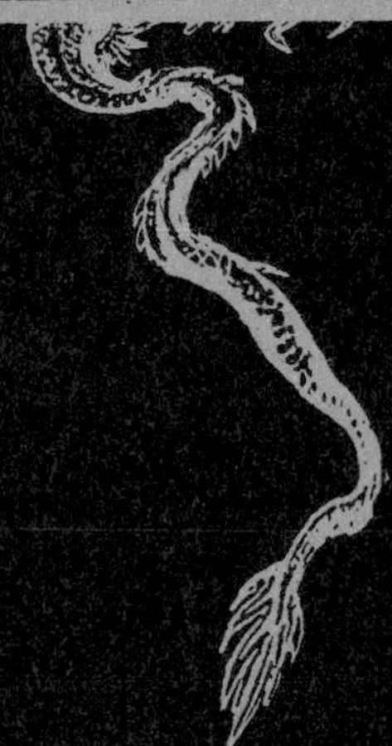

THE NEW YORK TIMES BEST-SELLING GRAPHIC NOVEL ADAPTATION
NOW COMPLETE IN ONE VOLUME!

DENISE **MINA** LEONARDO **MANCO** ANDREA **MUTTI**

STIEG LARSSON'S

AVAILABLE NOW